A Taekwondo Bond

The Spirit Within

R. Shane Murray

Contents

Dedication

To my dearest father,

You have been the guiding light on my martial arts journey, from that humble basement dojang forty years ago to every triumph and challenge since. Your unwavering support, enduring strength, and boundless love have shaped me into the person I am today. In every lesson and every hardship, you've shown me the true essence of martial arts—not just kicks and punches, but resilience, honor, and perseverance.

You are more than just my father; you're my mentor, my rock, and my best friend. Through life's darkest moments, you've exemplified the warrior spirit, rising above adversity with grace and courage. Your teachings go far beyond the techniques of taekwondo; they encompass the values of integrity, discipline, and compassion.

Thank you for being my constant companion on this journey, for believing in me when I doubted myself, and for instilling in me the wisdom that surpasses any martial arts training. With every step forward, I carry your legacy in my heart, knowing that your love and guidance will forever be my source of strength.

With deepest gratitude and endless love,

Shane

Acknowledgments

The late Grandmaster Byung H. Choi, my taekwondo instructor and friend, deserves the first and deepest gratitude. Beyond teaching me martial arts, he imparted invaluable life lessons and instilled a moral compass that guides me. A true pioneer, he brought taekwondo from Korea to the United States, shaping countless lives along the way.

I also extend my heartfelt thanks to the founder of Combat Hapkido and my Grandmaster, John Pellegrini. His mentorship and encouragement pushed me beyond my perceived limits, guiding me to accomplish more in my martial arts journey.

To my beloved wife, Nicole, your endless love and support have been the bedrock of my endeavors. You embraced my passion for martial arts as if it were your own. Your recent achievement of earning your black belt stands as a testament to your dedication and perseverance. Together, we have embarked on this journey, hand in hand, overcoming obstacles and celebrating victories side by side. Without your unwavering dedication and shared enthusiasm, this book may still have remained a dream. Thank you for everything; I love you dearly.

Special appreciation goes to my mother, who selflessly supported my father and me in our shared passion for taekwondo. Enduring countless discussions about martial arts at home and graciously giving up her time, she never showed jealousy towards our bond. Her constant and unwavering support has been a source of strength and encouragement throughout my journey.

And last but not least, to my kids Colin and Lyvia. It is because of you both that I continue to pursue my dreams and live out my passion. As your father, I am driven to show and encourage you by example, striving to inspire you and demonstrate that you're never too old to start anew or dream big. My deepest wish for you both is to discover what ignites your soul and to pursue it relentlessly.

About the Author

In the serene hills of upstate NY, nestled among the trees, resides a true martial arts luminary. As a Grandmaster in taekwondo and Senior Master in Combat Hapkido, his expertise is matched only by his passion for teaching. Alongside his wife, they run a renowned martial arts school, shaping the next generation of warriors. His journey has taken him to martial arts ceremonies worldwide, culminating in a prestigious honor- the induction into the International Spartan Hall of Warriors in the Canary Islands- for his lifelong dedication. His legacy extends far beyond the confines of the dojang, inspiring all who walk the path of martial arts.

Chapter One - In the Beginning

My childhood starts off like many others. I grew up in a middle-class family in an upstate rural area. My mother was the primary caregiver and disciplinarian of my sisters and me. She cooked and cleaned and made sure we ate and did our chores. She also worked weekends to help pay bills as money was tight. I'm sure many days, she felt like a single mom raising us because my father worked a lot. My father worked shift work at the local mill and often was gone fifty to sixty hours a week. His rotating shift meant some weeks he would be sleeping all day so we had to be quiet when we were home. Other times, we just knew we wouldn't see him at all after school when he was on second shift. When he was on the day shift, we actually got to see or spend time with him after school unless he got stuck working late because his relief didn't show, which meant he would have to stay and work overtime. Since money always seemed to be tight he took overtime whenever it was available as a means of one day getting ahead. He devoted most of his life to the local paper factory that didn't appreciate what he did and was in constant battles with his union for renegotiations every few years. Union discussions were a regular topic of conversation, and grievances with the company were a constant refrain. However, when it was time to work, he consistently put in extra effort, determined to secure a better future for his family.

I grew up with two sisters, one older and the other younger. I was sandwiched between the two girls. My oldest sister learned dance through her childhood and into her teens. This meant she would often come home and show off her newly learned skills for Mom or when company was over. I would always get roped into a small part in these productions. I would go out and make a fool of myself since I had no skills or rhythm whatsoever but we had fun entertaining and making everyone laugh. Not only was I surrounded by women most of the day but I grew up in a house of hairdressers. My oldest sister learned cosmetology in high school. She decided to learn this as her trade growing up, preparing for graduation and entering the workforce, and she still does hair today. About the same time my mother decided to go back to school to also learn cosmetology. So they learned together and from each other at times. The house was filled with hairstyling lessons and techniques as mannequins were attached to kitchen countertops, with supplies and products scattered all over many days. My youngest sister would eventually follow suit as she was surrounded by it growing up, and the general curiosity of the youngest sibling would intrigue and excite her, seeing the skills of my mother and older sister as they progressed toward their licenses. Curlers, hair dyes, and perms were part of my everyday life, and I often became a guinea pig when they had to learn a new technique. I was always up for the latest trend in hopes of fitting in with the kids at school. I had a tail when that was a popular fad and had it dyed blonde to make it stand out in my thick head of bushy brown hair. I also had a hair spike that was frosted on top when that was a cool trend. My hair was so curly and bushy it never looked much like a spike but I tried to pull it off. Years later, it was racing stripes down the side of my head to stay with the changing times. It was easy to stay abreast of the latest trends since that was the ladies in my family's profession. I didn't mind them experimenting on me because I was always on top of the latest fad, and finding friends and fitting in was important to me at that age. My sisters and I all got along; my mother made sure of it.

Being sandwiched between two girls as the middle child might make you think I took on their identities or got blended in the middle child role, but the truth was I was trying to find my way by learning about theirs. I was different than the girls and liked that I stood out in my parent's eyes. I was the boy, and it always made me stand out and feel special. My parents loved all their kids, and we all certainly each had special places in their hearts at different times, but it was clear that as the boy, I stood out. I was the one meant to carry on the family name. My grandparents also passed on their traditional values, and carrying on the family name meant so much to their generation; therefore, it seemed important to my parents as well. I was named after my father so the family name would carry forward, but I was called by my middle name to be unique and not be confused with him. This caused great confusion in school and with my friends growing up. So, I had to tell the story of why I was called by my middle name hundreds of times over the years.

My Dad worked a lot, and we didn't see him much during the week, but he always made time for the important stuff. My father made it to several high school football games when my sisters decided to become cheerleaders. He attended dance recitals and was very active in any event he could make. This often meant switching shifts with a fellow worker so he could be off or working extra overtime so he could leave an hour or two early. Somehow, he managed even when it wasn't easy. For me, he was my little league coach for many of my elementary school years. He was also my basketball coach during the years when I decided to participate in that. He was a cross-country coach for my sister's school team. She took up running because he was a runner, too. We all took after him and became runners at one point. My father was always goal-driven. He set his sights high and always achieved. He decided one day he wanted to run a marathon. He set the goal. He began training, and within a short time, was running 10 miles or more in preparation. He signed up for the closest marathon and eventually made his goal a reality. He walked away with injuries that would prevent him from doing that a second time. He was not only present at our events, but he wanted to be involved as much as he possibly could, no matter how much switching or overtime at work caused him. It didn't end there. He would be dead tired from working a sixteen-hour shift, but if I asked him to go out and throw the ball or play a quick game of hoops, he would always make time, even if it meant missing a couple hours of rest and going to work exhausted the next day. I experimented with many different sports like most young boys, and no matter which I tried my father was there and supportive.

I had previously played intramural basketball for a few years, Little League baseball for many years, and even tried two seasons of Pop Warner football when I thought that was what I wanted to do. I would try any sport because that's what friends my age were doing. I had enjoyed all these activities but never considered myself a star athlete. I didn't see myself playing professional ball in any of these events ever in my future. I realized there's such a small percentage of boys that possess the skills to play college or professional sports, and I realized I wasn't one of them. I definitely didn't excel at any of these activities, but they were what most boys my age played and who likes to be different? I spent elementary school trying to find my thing. I was slightly overweight, and always felt awkward and uncoordinated, so sports required a lot of hard work and practice. To me, at that age, like most, fitting in was more important than what I was doing, so school-related sports and activities were how to do that. I never really felt like I fit in, but I certainly tried in any way at that age to make that happen. One day, fitting in with the boys suddenly seemed to be temporarily less important when a cute girl named Stephanie from my class got my attention. She was genuinely nice to me. She was nice to everyone. She was always kind. I developed a crush. I loved the attention and was thrilled when she showed interest in me. She was so beautiful and full of life, and even at a young age, I felt we had a connection. We talked and joked and laughed and I tried to find ways to spend more time together. I made it obvious to her that I was interested. She took notice and began to get giddy and flirty around me. Unfortunately, my attraction to her had become obvious to the rest of the class too. I found out she had a big brother just two years older than me. Word of my crush had gotten around the school. Her brother found out, and he didn't like the idea of some boy showing interest in his little sister. I mentioned it to her, but she didn't seem alarmed explaining big brothers are just overprotective like that. So I wasn't concerned either. Turns out, since he went to the middle school across town, he had spoken with another boy from my class, and they decided to send me a message. It became the talk of the class, and suddenly, news made its way back to me. Panicking, I didn't know what to do. I didn't even know what this message meant for me. Would it be him asking me to stay away? I didn't think he'd resort to violence because it wasn't really any of his business. I was confused as to why this was such an issue for him in the first place. I grew up in a house of girls, so there was never any violence or roughhousing, and I never thought liking a girl would ever come to that anyway. Her brother was in middle school in a different building a few miles away, so he was not an immediate threat to me, nor would I believe anyone would try something on school property. So I decided to avoid any conflict that day and hurry home. The bell rang, and I grabbed my backpack and scurried out the door on a mission to walk home as soon as possible. Unbeknownst to me, he had asked that boy from my class to follow me on my way home. He ran after me across the parking lot. As I turned to notice, he jumped me from behind and tackled me to the ground. He held me down and punched me repeatedly in the face over and over. I struggled to get up but couldn't. He was bigger and stronger and had pinned me down on my back with his knees as he reigned punches down over and over on my face. I had no answers and couldn't move. I attempted to pull his arms up and hit him back but could only get a swing or two in from my back not delivering any noticeable damage. When the pummeling stopped, and I looked up, all I could see through my blurry eyes was a mob of my classmates hovering around me to get a glimpse, including Stephanie. After just a few minutes, the principal came running out from the school into the yard and broke up the fight by pulling us apart. I had been humiliated in front of the whole school, and my swollen and bruised face was not as damaging as the humiliation I felt in front of my class and her. I stood up, embarrassed and crying and hurried home as quickly as I could to continue my long walk home. I played the scenario over and over in my head as I walked. I couldn't believe this had happened to me. I couldn't figure out why her brother didn't like me or why he would recruit one of my classmates to do his dirty work. I had no clue what I'd done to deserve this treatment. As these and other questions swirled in my mind, I tried to pull myself together as I reached my driveway.

Too embarrassed to tell my parents, I rushed to the bathroom in an attempt to assess the damage to my face in hopes of finding a way to cover it up before anyone knew. I quickly said "Hi" to my mother and I put my head down and scurried towards the bathroom. Once in front of the mirror I knew there was no way I could hide this. The swelling and bruises had already set in, and my eyes were starting to close. My rushing into the bathroom alerted my mother, who immediately followed me to see what was wrong. Trying to downplay and hide the obvious, I started to say it was no big deal. Seeing how bad my face looked, she dug deeper into the line of questioning and would not stop asking. Trying to fight back the tears from my embarrassing encounter just caused them to roll out, and I slowly told the story, gasping as I spurted out the details of the whole encounter.

I continued to tell what happened and the who but didn't mention the sweet girl who was the topic of the incident. My parents picked up the phone and quickly called the boy's parents to have a sit down with him and the family. Like I wasn't embarrassed enough, now I had to confront my assailant face to face, knowing he had gotten the best of me. My parents took me and my swollen face over to their house, and I had to again describe the happenings move by move, blow by blow. I was humiliated! And although their intentions were to get some justice it made me feel more like a helpless victim as I couldn't stop them from trying to help. The school got involved because it had happened on school property, and the principal dealt him his punishment. The boy's parents were friends of my parents, and his parents were very angry and upset. They forced him to apologize, and even though that was supposed to make me feel better, it didn't. I felt more beaten down and humiliated as a result of the giant production this whole incident had become.

I returned to school the next day with two shiners. The event had become the talk of the entire elementary school, and when I thought I couldn't feel any worse I now knew that everyone knew of my humiliation and defeat. This single event would eventually be forgotten by most, but it stuck with me forever and shaped my life for years to come.

So when the *Karate Kid* movie came out in 1984, it inspired me to want to learn how to defend myself like thousands of other kids my age. Having been jumped, beaten, and embarrassed in front of my elementary school was the underlying catalyst and driving force to seek out a karate school. I dropped out of football and asked my dad to find a karate school. I believed that if it helped Danny, I hoped it could do the same for me. I was determined to never let this type of humiliation happen to me again. My father knew the underlying reasoning; how could he not, after such recent events, but he never mentioned it to me. The search for a karate school began. My father talked to a few friends at work in hopes of finding a school nearby since dojos (or dojangs) were not so prevalent yet in this country. The *Karate Kid* movie featured glorified training centers like the Cobra Kai dojo, but none yet existed in our area as far as we knew. My father learned from a friend at work that another coworker ran a small karate program out of his basement. It was a little off the grid and not the fancy Cobra Kai dojo I was expecting, but he took me to get started. So, a day of training began in a dark, dingy training area with worn carpets, one duct-taped heavy bag, and a handful of adults and a couple other teenagers. Not knowing what I was doing, I followed the strange routine not that different from warm-ups I had previously encountered in other sports. I knew I could do the movements, but it felt awkward and weird seeing all these adults and teens dressed in what could most closely be associated with pajamas. I had little self-confidence at the time. Recent events had certainly crushed the little self-respect I had prior, and starting something new wasn't easy for me. I managed to get through the routine and the strange motions that were expected of me, but I really didn't enjoy my first class. I already wanted to quit. I had only been to one class. Deep down, I hoped this was a better way to be prepared should another situation arise in the school yard. I had no idea how much this was costing my father, so quitting after just one class seemed out of the question—I couldn't bear to disappoint him. Instead, I resolved to stick with it, at least until I learned how to fight. The story almost sounds cliche knowing so many people who have begun martial arts for similar reasons. I went back to class, and after only a few months of practice, I was ready to test for my yellow belt so I could attend my first tournament. I was anticipating it'd be like a tournament scene from the movie.

Chapter Two - Maybe I'll Try

The martial arts school (dojang) that I had been attending was run by a husband and wife team; their names were Tom and Kathy Hammond. They were both black belts. Mr. Hammond was a third-degree, and Mrs. Hammond was a second-degree. Their home's basement served as their school, featuring concrete floors and walls, and a low ceiling supported by metal posts in the workout area. To soften the harsh surface, they laid a thin carpet directly on the concrete, albeit without any padding. It also helped make the concrete less cold and hard on bare feet. There was an American and a Korean flag hung lengthwise on one wall. A heavy canvas bag hung from the center of the room between the two support posts. There were only a handful of students as space was very limited. There were two other men around my father's age and three teenagers. It wasn't until a few months into our training that I heard the term taekwondo used during a class. I asked, "What is taekwondo? I thought this was karate?" My instructor, Mr. Hammond, explained that taekwondo was just Korean karate and that most people were familiar with karate because it had been around longer, but taekwondo was relatively new to this country and less familiar. Mr. Hammond was always full of energy and surprises and often wore a bandana across his forehead like martial artists you'd see in movies. He loved to spar and be aggressive and was very good at bringing out the best in everyone. Mrs. Hammond was more laid back but very detail-orientated. She often taught the poomsae (kata) because she enjoyed them more and paid more attention to each detail necessary to make us better. Her classes often focused on extensive stretching exercises different than those of her husband. Both made references to their instructor they called Master Choi. We started every class with the same warm-up routine and then kicked for twenty to thirty minutes. Next, as a group we practiced basic movements over and over back and forth down the basement lengthwise. We practiced our poomsae together some times and individually other times, but in the last twenty minutes of every class, we sparred. Everyone loved sparring. Training in the basement was exciting. We toughened our body parts by smashing our hands using our knife hands. We punched each other hard in the stomachs to toughen our abdomens. We strengthened our legs and dulled the nerves by kicking each other in the shins. It was a routine I later saw featured in other martial arts movies as they kicked trees until they were strong enough to make the trees fall over. Training at the Hammond's prepared our bodies for battle. We got stronger and harder and loved the unorthodox methods used by our instructors. Classes with Mr. And Mrs. Hammond were on Tuesday and Thursday evenings for ninety minutes, and then on Saturdays, we were expected to go to their parent school, Choi's Taekwondo Academy. The Hammonds had a special arrangement with Master Choi to be able to teach classes and open their own school as long as all students attended Saturdays at Master Choi's school. In this arrangement, Mr. Hammond was the designated instructor for classes at Choi's every Saturday. On Saturdays, the entire class would attend class at Choi's Taekwondo Academy in a neighboring town. Classes there were different than in the dingy house basement of the Hammond's house. The dojang was much larger, with newer carpets and real kicking pads and hanging bags. Master Choi had many of his own students, so we were exposed to sparring and poomsae with more than just the few in the Hammond's basement. I learned from having to interact with these additional students and seeing how structured and disciplined the art was in a larger group structure like his. Master Choi very seldom ever taught. I rarely saw him since he left Saturday instruction in the hands of one of his highest-ranking black belt, Mr. Hammond. I worked hard, learned everything asked of me and earned my yellow belt after just a few months of practice. There was no official belt presentation or special ceremony. I just tested on a Saturday at Choi's Taekwondo Academy and was told to go home and die my white belt to yellow. Once dyed and dried, I could return to class the following week wearing my new color.

Once a yellow belt, I was ready to attend my first tournament. I was very excited. The Hammonds did extra practice in class on my designated poomsae selected for the competition, and I did lots of extra sparring. Master Choi always offered extra classes at his school to ensure his students were ready for competition. I attended them all. He would come out of his office to offer pointers and criticism. I could tell my performance would be a reflection of him and his teachings at the tournament. He wanted me to look good and do well. I practiced diligently after all regular classes and stayed late for further observation and constructive criticism. I eventually attended my first tournament, expecting it to be like the scene from the *Karate Kid* movie. The experience turned out to be extremely exciting and invigorating, being my first time, but it turns out it was not much like the movie at all. My division only had a few competitors my age and rank. The sparring competition was much more intense than sparring practices, and the poomsae competition was nerve-racking. When it was over, I walked away with a couple gold medals and felt great about myself. My father took me to my first tournament and sat and watched in amazement.

My father was a huge boxing fan when I was growing up. He not only watched the fights but liked to twist and nudge with each fighter's movements and seemed to be the arm chair corner man and commentator both at the same time. Since I was not old enough to drive, my father drove me to every karate class. He sat on the side of each class, watching. He always had plenty of comments, suggestions, and criticisms after each sparring session like it was a live boxing match. It was frustrating being told what I should have been doing differently. The car ride home was often filled with these talks until one day, I had had enough and spoke up and blurted out in frustration, "If you think it's so easy, then you try it!"

He sat back and thought for a second, not sure to be angry at me or not. He was certainly surprised by my outburst and calmly responded, "Maybe I will" and so his journey too began. The next time he took me he started taking classes together with me instead of sitting on the sideline. He realized quickly it was not as easy as it looked. He began to understand that there are so many moving parts happening in any poomsae that it's super hard to concentrate in order to understand well enough to perform. When it came to sparring, he thought it was a boxing match, and he was always looking for a knockout. He used mostly all punches and attempted to hold his own this way for quiet a while since he hadn't yet developed any kicking skills. Class was not enough practice for either of us. We felt like it was a race and needed to develop our skills quicker to be able to not look foolish in class especially since all the other students had more experience than us. We started practicing together at home in our one-car garage. It was dusty and dirty and very small. My father was always building things or repairing things so the garage had tons of tools and saws and scraps of wood from various projects scattered all over. We had to clean it up and move things around a bit just to have enough room in this very small one-car garage. The garage had no heat, and we had no equipment, but it was the only space we had at home large enough to practice. We had to dodge some of the obstacles, like the snowblower, lawn mower, rakes, and shovels, among other miscellaneous items. We did basic movements back and forth over the cracked, uneven concrete floors in shoes so our feet didn't freeze in the sub zero temperatures. We wore jackets over our uniforms so as to not freeze to death. We attempted to replicate the poomsae and movements from our classes in the garage. I was one belt higher, so I was always the teacher. I was only a yellow belt but that one promotion had swelled my head and had given me the confidence to prove I knew more. I loved to share my newly gained knowledge with him whenever I could. I had only started a few months ahead of him, but I knew more and felt like an expert sharing my knowledge with him, the novice. He was in his thirties at this time, and things didn't come as easy to him as they did for me. But I was young and cocky from my few months of advancement, which made my lessons and teachings harsh. I wanted him to succeed but didn't make things easy or take into account that his age or abilities were different than my own. I pushed him hard, and he often got frustrated but ultimately found ways to overcome and endure the lessons. Our garage lessons often ended in an argument and him throwing his hands up wanting to give up. Deep down, a part of me didn't want him to succeed since this was my thing, after all. After only a few short months, I thought I was pretty good at being a teacher. He struggled at remembering the movements and had no flexibility, so I didn't see him sticking with it very long. I knew I was better, caught on quicker, and was much more flexible. But I was too young to realize these were all a result of my youthfulness.

Our garage lessons continued for several months and I had finally hit an obstacle in my own training that I was having trouble being able to overcome. It was the jumping, spinning crescent kick. I was shown in class but just couldn't understand how to make my body do what it needed to do to make this work. I got very frustrated. My abilities were hindered further by my frustration. Dad suggested I take it to the garage and practice it. What a great idea, I thought, but we didn't have a heavy bag or anything but each other's hands to kick at, so I wasn't sure how this might work. We really didn't have the money for a fancy heavy bag or kicking shield, but my Dad came up with an idea. He took out the ladder and climbed into the poorly lit attic as I held a flashlight. He rummaged through old cardboard boxes until he pulled out an old green Army bag. It was his old bag from when he served in the U.S. Army. He had remembered he had it and realized it was almost the size of a heavy canvas bag. He took it to the garage, where he filled it from the sawdust that covered the garage floor. Once he filled it with sawdust, he rigged a couple of old chains to it to hang from the rafters. It was an eyesore, but it worked for now. He stayed in the garage this time until I got frustrated and angry because I still couldn't figure out how to perform this new kick. He left and went inside and left me to continue to angrily practice by myself. I would eventually figure out the kick, but this was the first time I could empathize with my father over his struggles. It wouldn't be the end of me being hard on him and expecting more than I should have, but for the first time, I started to realize he was truly trying his best each and every time he practiced.

We practiced together for several years under Hammond's guidance progressing at similar rates. Our bodies developed many visible black and blue's over the years to prove it. In those days, sparring was full force, and we were only occasionally asked to tone it down or exhibit control for fear someone would be sent flying into a concrete wall or metal basement post, which did happen on occasion. We did our poomsae and basic movements with the group as required. Poomsae were necessary to progress, but neither of us really enjoyed them. We saw some degree of relevance, as pointed out by our instructors, but we both really showed up to each class to be able to spar. Every block or kick we learned was a new skill to try during sparring.

Master Choi appeared to have a vast network of connections when we participated in tournaments. He seemed acquainted with numerous Korean school owners and was familiar with many event organizers. Later, I discovered that he was among the pioneering figures who introduced taekwondo to this country. He would often disappear at these events to converse with many of his Korean counterparts who had made similar contributions to the taekwondo movement in the United States. We had learned from Mr. And Mrs. Hammond that Master Choi was to be honored as the new head of the taekwondo AAU organization. This would be a prestigious honor for him and meant he would be able to help shape and guide taekwondo in the United States for years to come. The AAU tournament was the tournament our group most often frequented. Master Choi was dressed in a suit and headed to the AAU event to receive this honor. He drove an hour by car to the tournament. Several of us students were in attendance representing his school. Master Choi arrived at the tournament anticipating being recognized for this prestigious title, one that would put his name in U.S. taekwondo history. He would never receive this recognition for some reason.

After a few years of practicing, my skills had sharpened. It had been more than three years, and I was ready to test for a first-degree black belt. I was excited and nervous. I was more than prepared since my ego had grown immensely in just a few short years. On test day, I blew through every skill required of me like a professional while both my parents sat and supported me. After the exam, we all went out for pizza. My father was especially excited for me because he knew first hand how much hard work had gone into preparing for this event. He started to realize that his test for his black belt was just a few short months away. This created motivation in him like never before. There were many other adults around his age that had also joined at Choi's Taekwondo Academy so Saturday practice became a gauge of where he fit in comparison to others his age and skill level. This drove him even harder to prepare. He was determined to complete all the required materials, but he was motivated by wanting to look better than his peers. My father and I put in additional practice whenever possible to give us an edge over our peers. We started to become obsessed with taekwondo.

Back then, when the black belt exam was over, everyone went home. There were no formal presentations for your belt promotions or your accomplishments. When your test was over you didn't even know if you had passed or not. No one said anything good or bad. I knew I looked great on my test but there were no guarantees or anyone telling you, "You passed!" Instead, the tables were folded, and everyone went home immediately after the exam with no mention of either way. My father and I showed up to our next class and continued to practice the same things we had already learned. I was not permitted to learn new material until deemed worthy and awarded my new belt. A few weeks went by and still no black belt. Doubt set in. I knew I performed everything asked of me and did it well, but not being crowned black belt yet was very overwhelming.

My fellow students all assured me that I looked outstanding and had nothing to worry about, but I hadn't heard it from my instructor yet, so I became concerned and started to get discouraged. A few days later, Mr. Hammond came running into the dojang on a Saturday super excited, waving a black belt over his head. He rushed towards me and threw it across the room, exclaiming, "Here you go!" Now, it was official, and I tied it on immediately. I wore it proudly and was finally relieved. My concerns had suddenly disappeared. I was so excited I wore it all the way home and even laid it at the foot of my bed while I slept that night. I couldn't take my eyes off it.

My father worked hard for years but not without some obstacles. Master Choi had jumped in to teach at one of the Saturday morning classes when my father was there, along with a few of the other men his age. Master Choi was always short and, to the point, could express disappointment with just a glare. His look said it all. He didn't have to say a word. When he did speak, he was often hard to understand due to his poor English. On this particular day he noticed my father and a few others had kicks that weren't high enough. He looked at them shamefully and especially focused his eyes on my father. He walked over to the wall, drew a line on the wall over his head and said, "Black belts kick over the heads!" It was obvious it was directed at my father and the other men his age. Then Master Choi proceeded to say, "no kicky over you head, no black belt!" My father was months away from his black belt exam, and the message was clear. Being in his thirties and working a physical job all his life made him less flexible than me and other younger people. He saw this as a huge setback and was discouraged enough to want to quit. Some people are built differently. Flexibility is not the same across the board. It is obvious that the older we become, high kicking becomes more challenging. Master Choi and my father were about the same age, and Master Choi would demonstrate kicks over his head, but did that mean it was fair for him to ask, in this instance, to require everyone to do the same? I was concerned about the situation and didn't know how to help. But the Hammonds, who already had great high kicks, also got the message. As a class, we all spent additional time in the upcoming months to concentrate on additional stretching inside class and outside. We practiced high kicks every class to the point the tendons and ligaments in our knees and groin felt like they would bust. We added ankle weights to our leg raises to further stretch the already overstretched joints. We did partner stretching during class. My father and I spent our evenings in front of the TV with our legs spread apart, working on additional stretching whenever possible. We partnered up to push each other and make great strides in the short time we had before my father's test.

My father, determined, set the goal and did all the work to achieve it. His kicks had drastically improved, and he was kicking over his head. He was now ready for his test. My father tested and earned his first-degree black belt in taekwondo. All his kicks were well above his head that day, and from that day forward, we would never forget the lesson.

We both continued to practice for a couple years together as black belts until I was eligible to test again for my next belt. I was getting ready to head off to college soon. I couldn't wait to earn my second degree and hit yet another milestone before I even graduated from high school. I was very ready and couldn't wait. I showed up on test day and sat with my legs crossed on the ground. In those days, we sat until it was our turn to show our material. I sat and waited. I waited some more until Master Choi stood up and bowed and let everyone leave symbolizing testing was over. I hadn't yet done any of my new forms or movements and hadn't had an opportunity to spar or show anything. What was happening? Had I failed before I even started? Was there something I said or did that was not to his liking that caused me to be no longer eligible? I went up to him and asked if he had forgotten me. He said, "Oh Shanie, you get car and meet me at park." I had no idea what this meant but I hurried to my car and headed to the park while my family also followed. It turns out that weekend was "The Festival of The Arts" downtown, and Master Choi had signed up to do a martial arts demonstration. I was to be the focus of this demonstration. He had asked a few others, including my father to also come. My test was to be performed in the park on grass in front of hundreds of people attending this event. He had never had good luck arranging demonstrations. Coordinating dates and times, and making sure he had enough students for such a demonstration was challenging. So, to make sure he had at least one and maybe a few other students show, he saved my test for that day. I would have to perform in front of all these strangers. He knew my father and a few others would follow to watch, so he put them to work. I was extremely nervous and felt unprepared to be performing at such a big event, but I was confident I knew all my material and was ready to prove to him I deserved my second degree. The test went well, and I was pleasantly surprised by how exciting the whole experience was. I enjoyed the adrenaline rush it created. We would talk and remember this event for years.

One day in class, shortly after receiving my second degree, Master Choi called me out in the middle of the floor to demonstrate a technique. He would always ask someone with exceptional skills to take center stage to demonstrate so that all the others could aspire to what was being shown. It was my turn, and he rarely called on me. It was a simple front leg raise. I nervously took center while everyone stood and stared. I raised my leg up has hard and high as I could and fell backwards doing so. Embarrassed, I jumped right up to demonstrate it again, only to fall a second time. I was one of the highest ranks in class that day and let my nerves get the best of me. Master Choi only stared and pointed for me to return to the line. My face was red, and I was sweating. It was so embarrassing. He selected someone else to finish the demonstration. What a lesson in humility it turned out to be. My cockiness immediately faded away. I walked into class with my tail between my legs for over a month.

My father would be due to test a couple months later when he was eligible for his second degree. It was not a giant production in the middle of the park like mine, but my father always performed well. About this time we had begun to notice many of our fellow students that we met along the way slowly began to drop out. We were part of a select few that had stuck with taekwondo this long. With each progressing test, there were fewer and fewer of the people with whom we had started. We enjoyed being part of the select few, and we both loved to teach and share. We often talked of opening our own school one day like the Hammonds. We always joked about naming it Murray's Taekwondo & Pizza to Go. We both loved pizza, and it seemed to be our celebratory meal after big tests and events.

My father and I decided to attend another tournament together now as black belts. We were more experienced and more competent. There would surely be more competitors in the black belt division. That morning, as we headed out of the house my mother caught us as we were leaving with our bags in hand. She stops us and says, "Have fun, but whatever you guys do, don't spar each other!" We laughed and assured her that even though we were both black belts, we were in different divisions. I was in my teens, and he would be in the senior division, so there would be no chance of us sparring one another. So we headed out on our drive. Previously in class the competitive nature of the sparring would bring out the best in both of us when sparring each other. We were each driven to be better than the other, so occasionally, things would get out of hand. Arriving at the tournament as black belts, we were expected to judge the colored belt matches and grade their poomsae before it would be our turn to compete. This would take most of the day. It would be the evening before it was our turn to perform. I went first. I only had two other competitors in my division and easily took first place. Then, it was my father's turn to spar. He faced three opponents, dispatching the first two swiftly and effortlessly. The third was a giant. He stood at least eighteen inches taller than my father. He had a longer reach with both his arms and legs. It would be tough for someone like my father, who was mostly hands, to get in on him. I cornered for my father. Exhausted and battered, he asked for insight. I remember telling him, "You need to do something, Dad, this guy is killing you." My father became super aggressive as a result. He managed to take the victory. He had won his division, too. We both felt great but were sweaty and exhausted as we put our gear back in our bags. As we stayed to watch the other matches finish, we heard an announcement on the loudspeaker. There would be a special exhibition at the end and all participants were asked to stay. We were so excited. We thought we might meet or see a celebrity. We sat and watched as they cleared off all but the center ring. Everyone was now done for the day, and all competitors and spectators gathered around a single open mat. We excitedly looked around in anticipation. The announcer came on again and said the promoters of the event had noticed something when tallying scorecards. They had noticed that two first-place finishers only had a couple competitors in their age and rank bracket and, therefore, would each have an additional match to decide a victor. The announcer proceeded to claim that there would be a special father/son match to finish our evening and everyone was invited to stay. They called me out by name to the center. My father and I looked at each other. Then they called out my father's name, asking him to join the center ring. He approached the mat and all either of us could think of was that promise we had made to my mother that morning as we left. We couldn't let down this group of spectators and our fellow competitors. We were now stuck in the middle of the mat and asked to bow in. The match started off fierce as we quickly exchanged points back and forth. Everyone cheered us on. My father had improved a lot, and even though we often sparred in class, this was a competition, and we were both here to win. Our frequent sparring in the class had revealed each of our strengths and weaknesses to one another.

The referee stops us and calls out, "Sudden death, 2:2, next point wins!" In that moment, our years of training and sparring raced into my head, and I had to do something unexpected. I knew he would rush in quickly and aggressively to get close enough to make the winning punch, or was he thinking the same as I that he might try something I wouldn't expect? The referee yelled, "Sijak!" I wound up and tucked my leg as I spun into a reverse spinning sick kick as hard as I could, hoping he would get caught rushing in trying his punch. I nailed him dead center in the abdomen as his punch came rushing over to hit my chest. I was unsure of what the judges saw and what might be called. I looked up at my father, and he put his eyes down in disappointment, knowing mine would be the point called. We shook hands and hugged as everyone cheered on. We were told over and over how exciting it was, and many commented it was the best match of the day. Everyone was impressed, and no one could stop talking abut it. We turned out to be the celebrities that day.

After a couple years of my father and I going to classes together, my little sister also asked to join. She was six years younger than me, so the thought of having a kid in class didn't thrill me. Our classes were hard-core training. We smashed our arms and kicked shins. This was no place for a little girl. We broke boards with our hands and feet. Not to mention, at times, our sparring got out of hand, and someone would get hurt. This was definitely no place for a little girl. I didn't have much say in the matter. My father thought she, too, should be able to try. My sister, Sam, was carefree about her training in the beginning but loved to do the activities with our father and me. She worked hard and learned quicker than either of us. Her young, free-spirited mind allowed the movements to quickly be absorbed and applied. But when it came to sparring, she was still a little girl, and we were asked to go easy and be careful. To me this is not for what I had been training. I wanted to spar hard like we always had, so I went harder on her than most. I didn't want to give her a chance because toning down my skills was not what I had been preparing for these last few years. As a result of being surrounded by bigger, stronger men, my sister was forced to perform in class at that level, not that of a child. Sam eventually would become one of the guys. Her training with bigger, stronger men caused her skills to sharpen quicker. Her kicks were high because everyone in the class was taller than her. Within just a year she was hitting hard like the men. She participated in all the hard-core training rituals we participated in during class. She had become a force to be recon with in a much quicker time than anyone else I had seen in class. I was concerned she might be better than me one day.

We learned later the Hammonds weren't the highest ranking black belts under Master Choi. Our limited Saturday exposure had prevented us from encountering others until test day. When a black belt was being examined, it was in front of a panel of black belt judges, including Master Choi's elite. We met Greg Donahue, who wore a higher rank than both the Hammonds. We had only seen him on test days, but he seemed very sure of himself as he sat there judging.

We also met Tim Terry, who had another satellite school under Master Choi's guidance. He ran his program through a high school in another town on the outskirts of our area. We learned of Mr. Terry and his school when Master Choi decided to organize an in-house tournament at Mr. Terry's location. He rented out the high school, and competitors from Master Choi's location, the Hammond's school, and Mr. Terry's location were all invited to compete. Participants would compete in poomsae, sparring, and breaking competitions. Master Choi's other black belts served as judges. The tournament was one of my favorite competitions because almost all of Master Choi's students from all three locations turned out since it was local. Living in an upstate rural area, many students didn't attend the bigger tournaments because most were so far away and required long travel times.

"Shane breaking boards at Master Choi's tournament held in gymnasium hosted by Tim Terry"

One of Master Choi's other higher-ranking black belts that both Mr. Donahue and Mr. Terry admired was Frank Mulches. Mr. Mulches was a very large man. He didn't live in our area but he had returned to test for his next black belt with Master Choi. Frank Mulches was body guard and road manager for some famous singing duo. His taekwondo background allegedly landed him a career in personal security, and he was now traveling with the band. Mr. Mulches had come only to test. When he took the floor on test day, the entire place was silent. His feet pounded with every movement because of his mammoth size, but he moved gracefully and without a doubt. His yells echoed and shook the windows. It was the most impressive performance I would every see in that room. The only other time I would ever see Mr. Mulches was when he returned for a large demonstration Master Choi held at his school. Since Master Choi left instruction to his team of black belt instructors it was rare that we ever saw Master Choi himself perform. On this particular demonstration Master Choi had orchestrated something out of the ordinary for us to witness. He started with a difficult poomsae, one that none of us recognized. He looked amazing and flowed smoothly and gracefully, like I'd never seen in class. After finishing his poomsae, he walked out of the room for a minute and then returned to the center of the room with a small cloth bag with a string closure on it. He asked everyone to step back and poured the contents of the back on the carpet floor with Mr. Mulches by his side. He handed a stack of boards to Mr. Mulches to hold as Master Choi prepared. He had poured broken glass on the floor in front of him and was going to break the boards while standing one foot on the broken glass. He would do not just any kick but a side kick, which meant he would have to not just stand on the glass put pivot his foot while driving powerfully into the stack of boards with the other. I was shaking just thinking of it as he proceeded to put his standing foot on the pieces of broken glass. He moved his pivot foot a couple times to insure proper footing, and without practice or warning, he crushed the boards as Mr. Mulches held them. I was so impressed, but there was more. He had rolled a strange-looking device into the room. It was covered, so we couldn't see what was underneath. As he moved it into position, he unveiled a bed of nails.

This was the first time I had ever seen such a contraption. I only wondered what he had planned next. Master Choi removed his dobok top and laid it on the floor. He then went over and sat at the edge gingerly and proceeded to lay with his back on the bed. As he moved to reposition, I could see where the sharp needles indented his skin and left deep indentations. He moved a bit but eventually found the right position, and he laid still. I thought it was impressive but not something I couldn't have done myself by tuning out a little pain and spreading out the impact carefully. But it wasn't over. Mr. Mulches returned with a cement block and sledge hammer. Now, this was getting interesting. Mr. Mulches laid the cement block on Master Choi's belly as he lay still with his eyes closed. Mr. Mulches rose the sledgehammer up and then down to measure. He did it again, raising it up, and then he came down a little faster with this practice swing. Then, without notice, he slammed the sledge hammer into the brick as hard as he could while Master Choi lay underneath. The broken cement pieces fell to the sides. I was scared and shaking. There were tears starting in my eyes with concern for Master Choi. Mr. Mulches quickly brushed the remaining pieces away and offered him a hand. He slowly helped him up. I could only notice the deep imprints of the needles across this small man's back. I had never seen such a marvel. Master Choi hopped back to his feet and quickly tied his dobok back across his front as he bowed to the applauding and whistling crowd. It was the only time I would ever witness a demonstration of this magnitude for Mr. Mulches would never return to Master Choi's again after that. It was clear to all that Mr. Mulches was the only person he ever trusted to perform such tasks.

After approximately five years of practicing in the Hammonds' basement, they made the difficult decision to close their school. They had dedicated countless hours to training all of us and generously opened up their home to provide us with a space to work out. However, as the size of their basement class expanded, it became increasingly challenging to manage. Our harsh training practices started to pose potential problems in their minds since none of them had ever been asked to sign liability waivers. The realization of someone getting hurt on their property was a definite possibility, and even though we were all friends working towards a common goal, there was always the possibility of a lawsuit. Their small basement club that started off as all personal friends had grown to more than ten students regularly and the small basement now seemed too small. Plus, they had been doing martial arts much longer than all of us, and their priorities had started to change. The idea of giving up three days a week got to be too much of a commitment. They had a son and wanted to be able to spend more time with him as he grew up. So, they announced that their location would be closing, but we were all still students of Master Choi's, so we would be able to continue our training at his location without missing a beat. The timing of the Hammond's closure came only a couple months before my high school graduation. I was planning on attending college out of the area and practicing someplace there. So, the thought of continuing at Master Choi's school was an easy transition for my father and me.

Chapter Three - The Journey

When I arrived at college, my focus was on learning to live on my own and not on taekwondo for a while. My studies filled my days, while making friends and parties filled my weekends. I met a friend during my first couple weeks who had studied karate much of his life like me. We had several in-depth discussions about our martial art's journeys and how we got started. I never let anyone know of the incident in the schoolyard. It was something I kept close to myself and hid from others when explaining my interest in taekwondo. I simply explained that I was a result of the *Karate Kid* boom and, like so many kids my age, I ran out to find a karate school. He and I had a lot in common and didn't want our hard work and years of training to just end because we went off to college. So, we decided to exchange ideas and learn from each other. We talked to the directors at the college and got permission to use an empty classroom as long as university instruction was done for the day. We practiced our arts together: he focused on his kata while I performed my poomsae. Though we practiced separately due to our different styles, we later discussed the similarities and differences between them. We did basic movements and escapes on one another and saw the similarities between the arts. He had studied a Japanese style of karate that I knew very little about at the time, but the things we had in common outweighed the few origin discrepancies. We also sparred together in this abandoned classroom every time we got together. Both of us had brought our protective gear to the university in hopes of continuing our martial arts training. We had a lot of fun together, but with college studies and different schedules, we were not able to meet regularly. I wanted to have a real taekwondo school to practice at again. I did some calling around and found another taekwondo school not too far from campus. It was about two miles away, but I didn't have a car, so I walked down to check it out. The Korean instructor greeted me promptly with broken English, and I signed up immediately, asking no questions. I returned the following day for my first official class and stood in the room wearing a black belt. I was surrounded by all colored belts. I was the highest rank in the room besides the instructor himself. We bowed and signed in. He immediately began to yell out commands in Korean. I stood frozen, not knowing what he was saying, as all the colored belts around me began to move. I just tried to follow. He then yelled out another command again in Korean and I had no idea what he was saying. This went on for almost an hour. I was embarrassed and confused. I knew all the movements, but my instructors, the Hammonds, and

Master Choi, always commanded the movements in English, not Korean. It was a humbling experience as a black belt. Feeling emotionally defeated I started my walk home. It was after eight o'clock now and very dark outside. The two-mile walk seemed extra-long at this time of the evening. I returned a couple times, but the long walk to and from the studio in the cold was discouraging me. Showing up and not understanding the commands made me feel like a fool in front of all these beginners. I decided not to return.

When the first school break came, I was anxious to get back to classes at Choi's Taekwondo Academy. I hurried in not only to freshen up my skills but to see my martial arts friends. All of the familiar faces were there and happily greeted me and welcomed my return even if just for a few days. This happened most breaks, and over summer vacation for the first couple years I attended college. My father had continued with Choi's Taekwondo Academy while I was away.

The Hammonds were no longer active instructors and no longer active students with Choi's Taekwondo Academy either. They had taken time to focus on their family and hadn't continued training at all. Another higher-ranking instructor under Master Choi, Mr. Donahue, was frequently the head instructor. He was a long standing student and black belt of Master Choi's. He apparently started when Master Choi first opened the school along with Mr Mulches, Mr. Terry, and Mr Hammond. He had outranked both Mr. and Mrs. Hammond when they were still active. He walked with confidence in every step and brought the class to attention like a drill sergeant. Everyone respected him and his skills. His abilities spoke for themselves as he performed movements across the floor. He would start class each day with a similar lesson until Master Choi was free and able to come in and take over. Mr. Donahue taught the majority of the classes, and Master Choi usually appeared when there were only ten to fifteen minutes remaining in class. He would then fine-tune student's movements and referee the sparring matches. Some days, Mr. Donahue would have to run the whole class when Master Choi was talking to parents or potential students in the office.

As black belts under Master Choi, we were expected to teach. My father and I were no exception. We taught some colored belts at Choi's Taekwondo Academy. We would be asked to lead on occasion if Mr. Donahue or another higher rank wasn't present. There was a hierarchy, and we were taught to follow it. If you were the highest rank in the room, you were expected to get things started and lead. This hierarchy of rank also meant that if a higher rank asked you to do something, you did it without questions. That included teaching others during or before classes. We often showed basic movements to beginners before and after classes. We both loved to give back and teach as Mr. And Mrs. Hammond had done for us. Teaching taekwondo was not something either of us ever expected to do, but we both enjoyed it. It was a nice feeling to be able to get up in front of a bunch of people who were less experienced and be the expert for a moment. We both found the experience rewarding yet exhilarating. We both took the opportunity to teach whenever the opportunity presented itself. We felt it was our duty to Master Choi.

I looked up to and admired Mr. Donahue. He was a true leader in my eyes. He was confident and always sure of his abilities. I always enjoyed working with him since he had a vast knowledge base in taekwondo. He seemed to know more than anyone else in the room and was the most experienced student training under Master Choi. My father, too, looked upon Mr. Donahue and saw all the time and dedication that Mr. Donahue devoted to the students at Choi's Taekwondo Academy. No one there contributed as much of his time to Choi's Taekwondo Academy as he did. I was only home for a short time and would return to my world and leave taekwondo behind once college was back in session.

My father continued practicing at Choi's Taekwondo Academy toward his next black belt. He tested and received his next black belt during the years I was away at college. I was a little jealous because this made him a higher rank than me, but I was away at school not practicing any longer like him. My life had taken a different course, and taekwondo became less of a focus. My father definitely worked hard and deserved to be a higher rank than me now.

The next time I was home I returned again to classes. Mr. Donahue took the lead like most days. He stood up in front of the class and announced that he would be taking over Choi's Taekwondo Academy and moving across town. We were thrilled for him. He deserved it for all the hard work and dedication to Choi's. He was the logical choice for Master Choi to pass on the school. He had lots of knowledge and definitely put in his time helping Master Choi. This could only benefit us. He was a great practitioner and excellent instructor and much easier to understand than Master Choi. We were looking forward to the change. He also promised to bring in new poomsae, a bo staff curriculum, and weapons disarmament, all things we hadn't learned from Master Choi up to this point. My father and I, both being at black belt level, knew there was little new material to learn as black belts, according to Master Choi. Our class time at this point was spent instructing others or re-practicing the basic techniques we had already mastered. The idea of new materials was enticing. We helped pack up the dojang and move all the flooring and equipment to Mr. Donahue's new location.

My father was the biggest helper. He always gave his best when it came to taekwondo. He filled his car with as much as he could of equipment to help. He brought his tools and put up sheetrock for walls; he helped lay and secure the carpet. We made many trips and gave up our weekend to help Mr. Donahue move the school. We managed to get everything to the new place. To our surprise, the sign out front no longer said Choi's Taekwondo Academy. It now read Upstate Taekwondo and Hapkido. We weren't sure why the name changed but assumed it had something to do with opening a school in a different town, but we weren't sure. Master Choi had taught hapkido at his school but never publicized it. He had a few students who attended in a small semi-private classes. Master Choi claimed that it was hard to keep hapkido students because there were many injuries that occurred during its regular practices, so he didn't promote it. He only had a few taekwondo students who decided to dabble and explore hapkido. We thought, "Maybe Mr. Donahue was planning on offering hapkido too?" We weren't sure. We knew Mr. Donahue hadn't learned hapkido from Master Choi, so we'd wait and see.

Mr. Donahue later informed us that one of Master Choi's traditional hapkido students had agreed to run a hapkido program around his taekwondo schedule. Jim Nichols would be the head of this program. He was a former taekwondo black belt and one of the select few who learned hapkido from Master Choi. Mr. Nichols had started taekwondo about the same time as my father, and they were close in age. Mr. Nichols had hoped to expand the hapkido program into more. He had a handful of Master Choi's old hapkido students come with him and join. He recruited a few of Upstate Taekwondo's students whenever possible. He ran a very small class for a year or two without much success. He had hoped to increase hapkido enrollment but thought the problem might be the location. Mr. Nichols relocated to a busier street, attempting to start his own hapkido school separate from Mr. Donahue. Unfortunately, his effort was short-lived, and the school closed after only a year or two.

All of Master Choi's students came to the new school with Mr. Donahue, and most were excited about the changes and new things happening. Except, there was no Master Choi there any longer. When we asked Mr. Donahue why, he replied, "Master Choi had decided to move his school closer to where he worked to eliminate his commute." Master Choi worked over an hour away, so this answer made sense. We didn't pursue it any further. I was still attending college at this time so I tried the new school a few times but attended less and less as time went on. College had consumed most of my time during the year and I worked two jobs during the summers when I was home. My father embraced the changes happening at Upstate Taekwondo and Hapkido. He learned all the new poomsae that Mr. Donahue required. He became proficient in weapons defense and bo staff. He took on a bigger role as an instructor. He taught for Mr. Donahue and spent as much time there as possible. It wasn't just about the belt any longer. It had become something much bigger for him. It was his opportunity to give back to the students. He loved teaching and finagled his shift work rotations around so he could dedicate as much time as possible to teaching the art and sharing his new found love with others. He loved it so much that after a couple years teaching for Mr. Donahue, he asked to buy part of the school and become a part owner. Mr. Donahue had many students attending but had been having trouble making his business profitable. He was thrilled at the opportunity to get some help and find ways to make it more profitable. Mr. Donahue agreed.

My father became partners with Mr. Donahue at Upstate Taekwondo and Hapkido. He bought in for equal shares. He never researched the business thoroughly and found that the business had some debt he didn't know about. The moving expenses, remodeling, and some new equipment created credit card debt that he, too, was now responsible for. My father didn't let this discourage him he proceeded to devote his heart and soul to the art he now adored. Being part owner and having an equal say meant he could make necessary changes to make the business profitable again. And so his mission began.

My father had a knack for encouraging parents to join with their children. Since this is how he started, he believed all parents would want to do it with their children. He never let any parent stand idle on the sidelines. He talked to them about his experience and would coax them into signing up. About this time the martial arts industry had begun to change. There was an influx of children in taekwondo like never before. Since the room was filled with children this was my father's opportunity to expand enrollment by encouraging parents. His idea was a hit. Parents would bring their children in to learn taekwondo but would sign up themselves shortly after. Parents loved to have an activity they could do together with their kids.

One summer, I came home from college and was eager to return to the dojang knowing my father was now part owner. I rushed over to the dojang, expecting to find him. I entered the waiting area and saw a few parents sitting there while the room filled with this nauseating smell of smoke. I looked quickly at his patrons in the waiting area to see who could be smoking. None were smoking. I proceeded to the office and pushed the door open, hoping to find my father. Instead, I walked into some strange man sitting at his desk with his feet on the desk, smoking a cigar. This gentleman acted pompous and arrogant. He was talking on the phone and acted annoyed because I barged into the office. He was wearing a black belt with lots of stripes, so I decided not to say anything about his smoking inside. He was alone in an office that didn't belong to him. This concerned me. Not knowing who he was, I called my father immediately. I asked who this stranger was and why he sat and acted like he owned the place. My father proceeded to tell me he was part of this taekwondo organization Mr. Donahue had become affiliated with. I could tell my father was not a fan of this gentleman, but it was obvious by all the stripes that he outranked my father and Mr. Donahue. My father explained that he was one of the individuals who had brought Mr. Donahue the new forms and new techniques he had been learning. I was glad I didn't say anything to him about the smoking so as to not ruffle any feathers of this senior black belt. I was still shocked that he had the nerve to be in someone else's office like that and smoking inside. I realized that they somehow needed this affiliation even though they may not have liked him very much or the things he was doing.

Once I completed my college education, I immediately started a family and career. These responsibilities didn't allow me time to get to continue with taekwondo classes. I worked twelve-hour shifts and rarely saw daylight. Taekwondo had no longer become my priority. My family and job responsibilities seemed to be more than enough to keep me busy. I dedicated my energy to my career and building a family. The little time I had left at the end of the day was filled with changing diapers or rocking an infant to sleep. I was physically and emotionally drained and had no energy left for anything or anyone else.

I took my children over to my parent's house every holiday and for family events whenever possible. My father would somehow always turn the conversation to taekwondo. He never stopped. I hadn't done taekwondo in a few years now, but every holiday and family function spent together meant my father spoke of his life as it pertained to taekwondo. He was obsessed and couldn't wait to tell me about the new happenings and the new students. He was excited to discuss his investment in half a martial arts school. I was happy for him. However, at this juncture of my life, taekwondo wasn't my primary focus. I had more pressing concerns, such as managing bills and raising children. Not a holiday went by without taekwondo talk, and my father questioning me, "When are you coming back?" This continued every holiday and every family function for years.

There was a four-year gap after college, and I didn't practice taekwondo. It had been eight years since I had been to regular classes because of college. Yet, every time I saw my father, no matter the reason, he would repeatedly ask, "When are you coming back?" He was relentless.

One day, aggravated by the repetitive question, I snapped back, "Fine, I'll come back!" I'm not sure if I had some deep-down desire to return or just got so sick of the questioning me, but I had finally succumbed to the pressure. But, I had conditions.

My employment had changed about this time, and I hoped that my new work schedule would allow for extracurricular activities again in my life again. I took a look at Upstate Taekwondo and Hapkido's current class times and realized their class times would still not allow me to participate. All his classes were done before I even left work. I had taken this new job in hopes of a better quality of life, yet I realized that most activities were still over before I arrived home. So, trying to please my dad and his request to return, I made a deal with my father and listed my conditions. Since he was co-owner of the school now, I would add three classes per week to their current schedule. I agreed to teach these classes for them and whoever might show up. I figured there had to be other people like me who worked late and couldn't make the earlier classes. But if no one showed up, I would have the floor to myself to practice.

Since I had been away, a lot had changed. taekwondo was marketed more to children so most classes had students ages 5-15. There were fewer adults. The adults participating were mostly parents of the children who had decided to try with their young children after gentle encouragement from my father. It was very different for me and not the place or art I had remembered. I remembered the day my little sister decided to join and how I felt. Now, there was a room full of little sisters. I wasn't sure if I wanted to continue because our hard-core training methods from my original days had fallen by the waist side. It had become a softer, gentler art because it catered to children. Some children were even younger than my sister had been when she started. I didn't understand what a five-year-old or even eight-year-old could get out of taekwondo. I thought, " Had they had a similar self-defense situation arise in their lives at such a young age that motivated them to join? How could they even effectively learn to defend themself when they just barely learned how to write?" I didn't understand, but I had made a deal with my father, so I stuck with it.

My return turned out to be not as easy as I had anticipated. Since I left, the school was part of a new federation, and all the poomse I had learned to achieve my black belt had changed and were replaced by different ones. I didn't know any of these new ones at all. Many of the techniques I had learned so many years ago had also slightly changed from what I remembered. So, there was a huge learning curve for me, and if I planned on "teaching," I had to take a crash course. Luckily, I knew a guy who was more than willing to help. My father was excited and eager to help. I asked him to teach me privately the things I needed to know. He agreed. He also was willing to work around my schedule to get me caught back up to where I was before I left. He willingly gave up evenings after regular classes to help me get started. I was still very limited in the times I had available because of my job and other obligations. I also asked him to meet me every Sunday afternoon. He agreed. He was willing to sacrifice Sunday NFL football games to devote the time necessary to get me back. He loved to see me back in it again, and we practiced for hours several days a week aside from his regular classes, including every Sunday during football season.

After several months of hard work and re-learning I had some regular students attending my new late classes. I loved being back and had forgotten how much taekwondo had meant to me. My father, equally delighted, enthusiastically shared news of my return with anyone who would lend an ear. Our family gatherings now involved engaged conversations about the current status of the students and the future of his business. I was no longer just listening to him talk about it. I was again part of it.

Most students preferred to still come to the regular class times that he had offered because they were just more convenient for most people who got out at a reasonable time during the day. The late class appealed to a very few who didn't have the luxury of getting out at a normal time.

Chapter Four - Be Careful of Betrayal

We had become close to Mr. Donahue and his family. I had attended high school with both his children. I had met his wife on several occasions. Mr. Donahue had attended my high school graduation, my wedding, as well as other events. We had learned a lot about each other's personal lives and struggles. He was someone who would listen. He often shared similar experiences in his life but would get back to business quickly, knowing that taekwondo was a much-needed distraction from life's problems. Mr. Donahue had embraced my return as much as my father did since we had started training together before I went away to college. He was thrilled to see additional classes added to their current schedule. My father and I spent countless hours in class and, after practicing together, each preparing for our next belts.

Many of the young students enjoyed attending tournaments. Being a black belt I figured it was a great opportunity for me to return to the circuit. I learned even the tournaments had become different than I remembered. The sparring had taken on new rules, and back fists to the head were now allowed. They previously hadn't been. Many of the matches were won with these jumping, flailing back fist attempts to the head. Many competitors relied on this one technique, and it often seemed like the only technique the judges ever scored. Competitors were often called for excessive force if one knocked the other down with a blow. It had become more of a game of tag now and less intense and physical than when we started. In my opinion, it required less skill and was less enjoyable. I no longer had an interest in competing as a result. There were large amounts of children now, more than ever in the past. There were children as young as six years old competing. These young kids would throw kicks and punches, and the fellow judges would ignore virtually every attack until one landed a jumping back fist to their opponent's head and suddenly the corner judges would call "Point!" I felt like an outsider at these tournaments because the rules I grew up learning were no longer. The massive amounts of children had overtaken these events and they better resembled a dance recital with children performing their body motions. Parents showed up to watch their children perform. Many were not competition material. Almost all went home with some kind of medal or trophy. They definitely weren't the events that Master Choi had previously taken us to compete in.

The new group that Mr. Donahue had become affiliated with was different than what we were used to under Master Choi. The senior instructors from this group wanted to be involved in any testing that happened at the school. Mr. Donahue had a new grand master to report to, an American, who brought his team of senior black belts in to conduct black belt exams and offer guidance and direction. They wanted things done their way with no exceptions. Mr. Donahue was allowed to run the school however he wanted to, but any technique or poomsae had to be sanctioned and approved by this new group. My father was due to test in front of this new team of black belts. The judges' panel was filled with all these high-ranking black belts with lots of stripes. All were Americans. My father didn't know many of these black belts but had to dress them properly and be respectful. My father took center stage proceeding to do the same techniques as he had been taught for years. They would stop him in the midst and make him repeat his technique. They didn't like something about the way he did it. They wanted to make sure he did it their way in front of everyone. They would call out random movement combinations in an attempt to make him slip or frustrate him. They would try to catch him off guard and make him repeat again. It seemed to me like they were just trying to discourage him. These black belts were attempting to embarrass him in front of everyone, including many of his own students. I didn't understand this new way of doing things. I didn't understand why Mr. Donahue tolerated this. He obviously needed them for something. My father endured the torture for almost four hours. It was a test that was meant to break him. He preserved and proved to me and everyone that he was a true warrior.

I enjoyed all my newly acquired knowledge in taekwondo through Mr. Donahue. However, since the sign out front still said, Upstate Taekwondo and Hapkido, I thought we should find a way to offer both. I reached out to one of my old taekwondo friends, Mark Steineger. Mark had practiced taekwondo under Master Choi for several years and had achieved his 2nd-degree black belt. However, shortly after Mr. Donahue took over the school, he had left taekwondo to pursue traditional hapkido. He had started his journey in traditional hapkido with Master Choi and then continued his teachings with Mr. Nichols when Choi's Taekwondo Academy became Upstate Taekwondo and Hapkido. He studied hapkido under Jim Nichols and moved when Jim had decided to open his own school. He and Mr. Nichols were very close from their years of practice together. He enjoyed taekwondo, and the knowledge he had gained made for an easier transition to hapkido, but hapkido was his new passion. When Mr. Nichol's program eventually dissolved, Mark wanted to continue training but was unable to locate a hapkido instructor nearby. So he decided to try his hand at the next closest thing and started learning aikido under a different instructor. I hadn't seen Mark in many years and didn't know if he still practiced either, so I decided to reach out. The phone call was a discussion of a lot of great times we had together in taekwondo over the years and the many friends we had made along the way. He brought to my attention that Mr. Nichols, who previously led the hapkido program, had passed away from cancer. Mr. Nichols had originally started off in taekwondo with us under Master Choi and had tested for his first degree with my father. We knew him well and remembered all the good times we'd shared together in class. After a few moments to reminisce I asked Mark if he'd be willing to teach me some hapkido so that I may start a program again at Upstate Taekwondo and Hapkido. Mark was thrilled and couldn't wait to get started. He hadn't practiced in many years and was anxious to get back into it. We decided to meet on Sunday afternoons and practice. Mark's skills were excellent. He was really good at explaining and helping me understand. However, it was challenging to retain, so I tried to record the movements on a piece of paper. There were so many moving parts that one simple escape would equate to a page or more of written explanation. It was tedious and time-consuming. I had mentioned the idea of bringing hapkido back to the school to my father. He was thrilled with the idea. He was excited to see if I could make a curriculum out of my pages of notes. Mark and I continued practicing and collecting data on paper for several months. However, something had happened in Mark's personal life and he would be unable to meet with me any longer. The pages of written content were mumbled and hard to understand without him there to explain and demonstrate. I learned several movements and escapes but didn't have nearly enough to put a curriculum together. The challenge loomed larger as there were no nearby hapkido schools that I could visit for additional guidance or resources. I unfortunately couldn't remember any of Jim's other students to be able to reach out to anyone else.

I continued to teach my three taekwondo classes a week and slowly became a bigger part of the school. I assisted at most black belt exams. Due to the changes in taekwondo all testing had become a big production. Students testing for their next color were awarded official looking certificates with a new belt in a big ceremony. Each student's family and friends would be invited so they may be present at the ceremony. It was nice to see candidates awarded for their achievements in a proper way differently than being told to go home and simply dye their belts. Black belt exams had become a long, grueling production, too. Candidates were expected to demonstrate every movement since day one including all these newly acquired materials not previously required by Master Choi. Mr. Donahue had acquired so much new material through this new organization that tests often lasted for four hours or more like my father's had. Black belt exams became lessons in fortitude trying to perform every technique.

My father poured his heart, sweat, and tears into his school. The business had grown, and it was time to find a bigger place to accommodate the growing demand. We all packed up our cars and helped move the school to a better location. This time on a main road in a much higher visible area. My father designed the new layout that would be conducive to his plan. The waiting area would be parent-friendly, with a large plexiglass viewing area. The waiting area would be near the office to make it easier for parents to make payments and buy equipment. The plexiglass allowed for viewing both ways so parents could watch their children, but he could always see who was sitting there waiting to be his next recruit. The new building had adequate changing areas and storage and was set up just the way it should be for the business to thrive. His partner, Mr. Donahue, was on board but not handy like my father so the design and much of the implementation was up to my father. Still working shift work, he spent his days off with a hammer and saw building his dream dojang. He had planned it and drew it. Now, he was building it. Many students helped out, and the project went very quickly. Once completed, he could stand to admire what a struggling business just a few years prior had become. The walls adorned with fresh paint, flags proudly displayed, and the introduction of authentic martial arts flooring instead of carpeting marked a significant transformation. It was a sight to behold and a realization of a long-held dream. He was on a busier road now. The place had more than ample parking. He was ready to roll.

The school still catered mostly to children. I started to adapt to the new way of doing things. So, I decided to succumb by enrolling my own children in classes. My son was older, so he started first and progressed quickly, earning his black belt in just a few years. Later, my daughter decided to join, and she would also earn her black belt eventually. There were tensions in my marriage due in part to the additional hours I devoted to my father's business, so having my kids there alleviated some of that. I finally involved my family in this art that meant so much to me as a teenager. To avoid partiality, I encouraged my kids to attend the earlier class taught by Mr. Donahue or my father. The early classes worked great with their schedules. Both kids enjoyed taekwondo for many years, earning multiple black belts as children.

Mr. Donahue had pulled me aside after a taekwondo class and asked me to practice a few new moves with him. Without question, I made the time. I was always excited to learn something new. The series of breakaways and escapes he practiced on me was similar to some we had done in taekwondo over the years but had a different flare. These side sessions with Mr. Donahue started to happen regularly, and I was more of a practice dummy for him than the student. He needed a body to practice on and I was it. He did pass along the techniques as best he could but it had become clear this was for him to be able to practice on me so he could learn these techniques better. I didn't care because I felt useful in this new discovery process and loved the little that I was learning in the process. The sessions became so frequent that they started to interfere with my family time. I didn't want them to end, but I needed to find a happy median. So, I asked Mr. Donahue where this practice was headed and for how long it would continue. He explained that he had sought out a hapkido program and had started learning from a group slightly outside of our area. It was about an hour's drive for him, which proved to be difficult because of the hours he put in running Upstate Taekwondo and Hapkido. But somehow, he was determined to learn and hoped to eventually bring it back to be able to teach. I was thrilled since I had been unsuccessful at doing the same thing just a couple years earlier. My discussion opened the door to his confidence. My excitement about this new art had sparked enough interest for him to start a couple hapkido classes during the week. He was eager to spread this newly acquired knowledge. He had secretly been belting in hapkido with this organization without alerting any of his students. He believed that he needed to acquire a few skills and start his progression in hapkido before he would offer it to others. His lack of time due to traveling an hour to learn from this organization meant he had to get extra practice on his own. This is where I came in. Our secret sessions were his opportunity to practice without the others knowing about it. Since I was one of the highest-ranking black belts in the school, he felt he could confide in his practice with me without judgement. He believed no one would want to learn from a master who didn't know himself. His point was understood, and it was nice to hear that the "…Hapkido" would finally again be added to fulfill the sign.

I wasn't sure if my father even knew his partner had started this new venture, so I decided to ask. He acknowledged that he had heard he was traveling a couple days a week to train but wasn't very familiar with the group or the new material. He sounded like he really didn't see it

33

taking off, so he was a little skeptical. He exclaimed this was Mr. Donahue's baby and that he would wait and see what, if anything would become of it. It was clear that he had no interest.

The new hapkido classes were added to the schedule. It drew in a few taekwondo students who wanted to broaden their knowledge and one or two outsiders who had heard about it from other members. The classes became a regular thing but never had more than four or five students at any one time. Mr. Donahue taught, and occasionally, he would bring his hapkido instructor up to offer pointers and further explain the techniques. Mr. Donahue strongly encouraged me to join since he had already shown me most of what he knew. He said it'd be easy. The work life balance thing had started to become a problem for me. I was concerned if I would be able to attend all the classes. To dedicate that much more time meant I wouldn't see my kids before bed. I was already teaching three taekwondo classes a week, so adding another two hapkido classes meant I wouldn't see them at all before bed during the week. I fought for that balance and agreed to attend just one of his classes per week. I progressed quickly since I had already worked on almost every technique with Mr. Donahue previously. Practices were fun but hard since they seemed to contradict some of the harsh principles I had been taught for over 20 years in taekwondo. There was something different about hapkido that intrigued me, and I wanted to learn more. So, I was determined to get started right away, working towards a black belt in hapkido. Mr. Donahue wanted me to progress quickly so he would continue to have someone with which he could practice. My one day a week slowly turned to two. I really enjoyed it and was learning so much. After a couple years, I had progressed to black belt in a very informal black belt test with a couple of Mr. Donahue's other students. His instructor had come up from his school to test us.

One day, Mr. Donahue received a phone call from his American taekwondo grandmaster. He had called to notify Mr. Donahue that he would no longer be practicing taekwondo. He had decided at sixty years old he wanted to go back to college and pursue a different degree. He wished Mr. Donahue and the school the best but would no longer be assisting them. Mr. Donahue was shocked. This phone call came without warning. He had learned all the requirements of this new federation and done all that was required of him and the school, but he would have to find a new affiliation. In order for him to continue to grow in taekwondo, he would have to seek connections elsewhere. If he was unable to grow and advance meant none of his students would advance either, including my father and I. Mr. Donahue would have to pursue a new grand master in order to eventually be able to progress. Mr. Donahue made many phone calls until he found a Korean grand master in the city, about four hours away. When he was eligible to test, he made the four-hour drive to an unfamiliar school expecting to meet with this new grandmaster he had never met in person. Upon arriving, the Korean grandmaster he spoke to on the phone was not there. He met with one of his high-ranking black belt instructors. He was asked to perform in front of this instructor instead. Mr. Donahue demonstrated his techniques and poomsae. His techniques were always flawless. However, he kept getting stopped and asked to slightly tweak each motion. The poomsae were also slightly modified. He was asked to change his movements to accommodate the likings of this new grand master. After a few hours of intensive criticism, he returned home. He was eager to spread these subtle changes with us. We were all asked to conform yet again to his new grand master's way of doing things. We were told that we all needed to buy this grand master's book. We needed a reference material to accommodate his way of doing things now. My father and I bought the book and immediately proceeded to share it again across the dojang with the other students. The message was that all very high-ranking black belts have a slightly different way of doing things that sets them apart from others. Therefore, they want their way to be spread and shared with all successors.

At about this time, my father was approaching retirement. He had had many talks with me about fulfilling his dream and devoting all his time to the martial arts school as he retired. Many years of shift work and hard labor had made it a struggle to dedicate as much time as he wanted to taekwondo. It was his true passion and he loved all the lives he had touched through it over the years. He encountered countless troubled kids, children with disabilities and learning impairments, and many parents that he had conned into joining with their children. He had definitely made an impact on the community while making numerous friendships and building bonds over the years. Yet, he wanted to give more and felt he would make a bigger impact if only he had more time to dedicate to the cause. The plan was in place, and the countdown started. He would retire early to devote more time to taekwondo. He had a calendar marked with the exact day he would leave the paper mill and become a full-time martial artist. The family all knew of his dream and so did Mr. Donahue and their students.

When the big day came, he was thrilled. He would finally leave the job he dreaded all his life so he could devote his energy to making the school even bigger. Mr. Donahue would no longer have to work around my father's shift work schedule. My father would be able to be there every day now. He retired and devoted all his time to teaching classes and the business.

He was now available to teach and be active in the business every day. Mr Donahue no longer had to accommodate my father's schedule. He could be there every day now. He and his business partner began to disagree on the future of the business. They had been partners for more than ten years. They tried to discuss the reasons openly, but that often ended in an argument. The disagreements became more regular and started to become personal. Both of their wives had been working in the office. They took payments from students. They sized up people for sparring gear. They prepared certificates and belts for test days. The school had grown, and additional help was needed to maintain order and allow my father and Mr. Donahue to teach. Soon, the job roles and responsibilities of one another came into question. The discussions turned to who's contribution was larger and who was in charge. Mr. Donahue outranked my father, so inside the dojang, there was no question who was in charge, but as equal owners in the business, they should each have an equal say in the future of the business. The taekwondo talks at our family functions between my father, and I became about the disagreements between him and Mr. Donahue. It was clear the partnership was under attack. My father had become frustrated that the business he had dedicated much of his life was now in jeopardy. I offered suggestions not really understanding the cause.

The tension between them was palpable, and it became clear to me they couldn't hash it out on their own. Taking my instructor, Mr. Donahue, aside, I respectfully requested permission to intervene. I proposed mediating between him and my father, hoping to facilitate a resolution. While he acknowledged my offer, he simply responded, "Things have already gone too far." I was shocked. I didn't really understand. I knew they weren't getting along, but how could things had gone too far? I decided not to press it any further, feeling it wouldn't help.

Mr. Donahue had hired a lawyer and started a legal battle trying to push him out. Since they were partners, I didn't see how that could be possible. My father had literally built that place with his hands and sweat. He took early retirement so that he could continue to build and grow it. Now, Mr. Donahue has decided he doesn't want to be partners? The legal battle went on for weeks. Mr. Donahue hastily said he would padlock the doors and shut the business down because he didn't care about it or anyone in it. My father cared for every single student there. Each had a special place in his heart. The thought of preventing the students from practicing because he and Mr. Donahue couldn't come to an agreement was absurd. My father cared too much to let anyone lock the doors and shut down his business. He spoke to my mother and was frazzled over the whole ordeal. The lawyers sent offers back and forth, but it became obvious Mr. Donahue just didn't want him there any longer. The offers were pathetic in the eyes of what my father had done to save the business when it was struggling. Every offer that came across was clear: it meant that my father and his family would no longer be welcome at Upstate Taekwondo and Hapkido. He talked to me about how outlandish the offers were. He described how it had become personal and how Mr. Donahue was continually insulting his character. He showed me the letters stating that the family would no longer be welcome at the school. He wasn't sure how it had come to this but didn't want the students to suffer. He wanted to continue to fight for the students but refrained from doing so. He eventually agreed to leave so none of the students would be involved. He also agreed not to open a school within five miles. It was a true test of his self-control. They parted ways. My father quickly grabbed his bag of gear and left behind all equipment, supplies, and students. Knowing there was a deadline on the agreement, he had to be out immediately. He didn't even have a chance to say goodbye to any of the students he cared about so deeply. I, too, hurried over to the school to grab my bag of gear, uniforms, and my children's belongings. Upon arriving, Mr. Donahue stopped me at the entrance. He came close to me and said, "You don't have to go. You and your children are always welcome here."

I was surprised he would even suggest such a thing. He made it personal. The letters clearly referenced my father's family. I was a little shocked but quickly replied, "And not go with my Dad?... I have to support my father."

He moved aside to let me by and just replied, "I thought so." Was he serious? I couldn't believe he'd even ask. I did love martial arts, and the thought of leaving that all behind was devastating, but family is family. I never really knew if he really thought my love for martial arts would win over my own father. I gathered my belongings and proceeded to leave. I did think for a minute about all the things I had learned while practicing there at Upstate Taekwondo and Hapkido. I thought of all the guidance and direction Mr. Donahue had offered over the years. I thought about how he went out on his own and took a chance to make the school into more. I wondered what this meant for my future. I left with my head down, wondering if I'd ever practice taekwondo or hapkido again.

My father's dream had been crushed! It couldn't have come at a worse time. He was finally retired and ready to devote his time and energy one hundred percent to the martial arts business and he no longer had it. He was sad and depressed. He was lost. He came over to my house night after night to talk about it. He wore his head down low and had no pep in his step any longer. He sat at my kitchen table, choking back tears night after night in the weeks that followed. I tried to console him but really didn't know what to say. He came seeking direction and hope that the dream was not lost.

I still wanted to practice, so I checked out all the other martial arts schools in the area. Most of the other schools were very small in comparison. Most had young, inexperienced instructors teaching, while the owners were rarely present. None offered 20 classes a week, like my father's school. All had separate children and adult classes, with an average of only 4-5 students active in any one class. None were the mega school Upstate Taekwondo, and Hapkido had become. I also learned that both my father and I outranked all the other school owners in our area. How could I learn or grow from a lower rank? How would I progress without Mr. Donahue? My father continued to come over to my house night after night, looking for hope.

Chapter Five - Building the Empire

After a few weeks of seeing him depressed, I had to say something. I finally looked and said to him. "Either you open another school, or I will!" He looked up like he had been waiting all this time to hear those words. I said, "Dad, either you open up a school, and I'll help you, or I'm going to open one, and you'll work for me."

He replied, "So you want to be partners?"

I said, "No, not partners, but I'll certainly help you in any way you may need but I don't want to be partners." It was really hard for me to say that because deep down, I did want to be partners, but seeing what had happened to his last partnership, I was afraid it would ruin our relationship. I was a manager at my job during the day. Business was business. I learned firsthand how personal involvement and family can get in the way of business decisions. I didn't want that to happen to us. So I offered to help and meant it. I meant that I would be his partner in teaching and operations, but when it came to financial decisions, I would leave that up to him since it would be his investment. I also knew my job would limit the times I could be there, and the majority of the class instruction would fall on him.

I told my father I had checked out all the other taekwondo schools in the area and knew what they offered for classes and pricing. I knew we had much more to offer from our experience and credentials. I took out a map and drew out exactly where 5 miles ended so we could begin our search. We started checking out storefronts just outside the five-mile marker. Rent was much higher than he previously paid and any place would need some remodeling. My father had very little money to get started, so I was concerned. He needed to buy equipment and flooring. He needed to cover his rent and utilities. He would incur new remodeling costs for any places we were looking. Plus, the five-mile radius put us into lower income demographics, so we were concerned if the clientele would be able to afford martial arts classes. So we headed back to the kitchen table for another discussion. I grabbed a piece of paper and listed all of his monthly expenses along with the start-up costs. Crunching the numbers, I calculated the exact number of students he would require just to break even, before he could even think about turning a profit. I did the exercise to talk some sense into him. I was concerned, after seeing all the other schools how he would get enough students to survive. All the other schools in the area had very few students in each class and I didn't know how they had afforded to stay open. I did the math and determined he needed forty to break even each month and that wouldn't cover his initial investment. My father was retired now. He was now on a fixed income, and he was looking at starting up a business with nothing. He had zero students signed up so far, so getting forty would be tough. Then I said, "Plus, Dad, we haven't even considered marketing costs or a website yet. You will need a website to be successful."

Without hesitation, he replies, "I can do it. We'll get forty students." He didn't understand my intentions here. I was concerned for his financial well-being headed into retirement. I could tell there was no stopping him. He had dreamt for years of running a taekwondo school throughout his retirement. There was nothing I could say that would change his mind.

It was summer, and he had not yet made a deal on a storefront. We, as a family, were getting ready to head to the coast for our yearly vacation. Every year, my parents would rent a place on the beach, and my sisters and I would rent places nearby to join them. We all brought our children to enjoy the beach and some quality family time together. This year would be no exception. It would be a nice break from the stresses of the business break up and give everyone time to clear their heads and decide if starting a new taekwondo school would be the right thing to do. My father agreed he wouldn't make a decision until we returned home from our trip.

We all sat on our first day on the beach, watching the waves come crashing in, similar to what we do every year when my father's phone rang. Our whole family was there on the beach, so he wondered who might be calling since we were all there? He answered the phone; it was one of his old taekwondo students from Upstate Taekwondo and Hapkido. This student and his family were all black belts, with my father and Mr. Donahue. He was not happy with things there now, and he and his three children wanted to know where he'd be opening a school. We hadn't discussed the idea of opening a school with anyone outside the family yet. We still weren't one hundred percent sure when or where it would happen. We wondered how he found out. This student just assumed that my father would continue taekwondo, and he and I would open a school someplace together. When they heard what had happened between Mr. Donahue and my father, they weren't happy and wanted to follow my father and his teaching wherever that might be. My father talked for a minute, then put his phone down and told us all who had called and that they wanted to know where we'd be because he and his family would follow. We all laughed about it and the timing of the call. It was a true compliment to my father that they wanted to follow wherever that might be. We went back to sitting in our beach chairs, trying to relax and ponder.

Less than an hour later, my father's phone rang again. This time, it's one of the female black belt instructors from the old school. She had started with my father at a self-defense clinic he had offered 10 years earlier. She had been a loyal student and instructor there since. She loved my father for his assertiveness and the passion he shared when teaching self-defense. She also called to ask where he would be moving. She, too, intended to follow. A few minutes later, the phone rang again. Another family of four called, asking the same questions. This happened all week. His phone was blowing up from many of his old students, wondering where he was going to be and how soon they could come. No longer was my father taking this week's vacation to think about it. His students had spoken, and now he was convinced it would be a success. It was just the push he needed. The entire vacation turned to discussions about location and which students would be there when he opened.

Upon returning from our trip, my father immediately called and made a deal on a storefront. It was exactly six miles away from the previous place. It was just outside the do not compete area. He bought equipment and mats. He furnished it with mirrors. The place was starting to shape up. I designed a Facebook page to be able to market his new business. He and my mother sat and discussed in length the new name. After tossing around several suggestions, they came to a conclusion: Murray's Family Taekwondo. Considering my father's widespread recognition among numerous students, they believed that his name should be included. He also thought it'd help more students find him. He had so much impact on so many people over the years that the name would bring in some more of his previous students. The Family part of the name was because he wanted families to be able to work out together in the same room, not segregated classes by age and rank like other places offered. He had always done so well encouraging parents to try with their children that this method would continue. They excitedly approached me about the name they had decided. I brought up that taekwondo would be too specific if we ever intended to offer additional arts. I suggested Martial Arts Center instead. I had fallen in love with hapkido and wanted to be able to offer hapkido classes, too. I also thought it would encompass any other arts if we decided to add more down the road. After a moment of discussion, the name was decided: Murray's Family Martial Arts Center. It was time for a grand opening.

I promoted the grand opening event on Facebook, and my father took an ad out in the local newspaper. I built a small business website as quickly as I could. The website was ready and he set a date for his opening. On the day of the grand opening celebration there were twenty people that showed up. Almost all were family members who came out to support my father. My father had also invited the Hammonds, our old instructors. They arrived with one of their early students from the basement days, Charlie, who was among their first pupils when they started teaching. Charlie and his son practiced together during our early years with the Hammonds. Charlie and his son were both someone my father and I both looked up to. We admired them both for their skills as higher ranks when we first started. Charlie was always eager to help us in those days and we learned a lot together. We had practiced together with Charlie and his son all the years the Hammonds ran their school. Charlie had continued with Choi when the Hammonds closed their school but eventually stopped when My Donahue took over. Charlie had also done hapkido with Master Choi when he offered it. Charlie had brought a gift for me. It was his old hapkido book from his training with Master Choi. It was ear marked with each belt requirement. He had heard I started hapkido and brought it for me to continue my studies. Besides the three of them at our grand opening, the only other people there were family members. I was discouraged. We received so many calls from students wanting to follow, but none were here. None of these people attending the open house had any intentions of joining. They all only showed up as a kind gesture to support my father in his new venture. Of course, I was doing the math. This wasn't a good start to getting the forty he needed to cover his costs. I was very nervous. Forty students was not going to be easy. Later that day, as we were getting ready to close the grand opening event, two of the families that had phoned while we were on the beach eventually showed up. They would be coming to train. I was still nervous because forty was still going to be tough.

Within the first month, news had traveled that the Murrays opened a school, and my father's phone continued to ring with additional students wanting to leave Upstate Taekwondo and Hapkido and come onboard with Murray's Family Martial Arts Center. It was the integrity he had carried within that attracted all his former students. He believed in what he did and the value of taekwondo. He believed that his students were most important. Within a month, he had more than the forty he needed, and they kept coming.

Shortly after the grand opening we heard rumors of another former student and black belt of Upstate Taekwondo and Hapkido that had left with intentions of opening his own place too. The area was already saturated with taekwondo school but this student already owned a business and could afford to build his own building to suit his needs. He built a state-of-the-art training facility equipped with a cage for mixed martial arts. He had fancy mats and all of the latest training equipment. He intended to offer taekwondo, boxing, and grappling classes. He had the financial means to be successful but not the knowledge or experience that we offered in taekwondo. But mixed martial arts was extremely popular and I was concerned that might pose a problem for us.

My father and I realized with this type of art, we needed to advance ourselves in order to be able to advance his students as they progressed. He had several black belts students that had came onboard from the previous school and wanted to make sure as they progressed, we'd be high enough rank to continue to help them advance. In order for that to happen, we both needed to keep growing in the art. We needed someone higher than us to be able to do that. Since Mr. Donahue and his affiliates were out of the question due to recent events, we had to look for someone else. My father and I discussed possibilities. We both only came up with one name. Our first call would be to Master Choi. We weren't sure if he even practiced any longer or still had a school, but we believed he still lived locally. My father made the phone call. Master Choi picked up the phone and answered in his broken English. He was surprised to hear from my father. They spoke for a minute. Master Choi didn't give him an idea if he was willing to help or not. He didn't even indicate if he was still involved in taekwondo. He just asked him to come down to his location in Loudonville. Loundonville was about an hour's drive by car. My father and I headed down together, not knowing what to expect. Master Choi's new location wasn't conducive for a business. He was located on the back of a building in a busy plaza with no signage from the road. The parking lot was hard to navigate. It took us a while to park because there were so many other buildings and businesses crammed together in this plaza. We had trouble finding his place. We weren't sure how potential students were able to find him either. We didn't see any signs anywhere. We proceeded up some steps to the second floor. On the back side of the building, we located a small wooden sign that read Choi's Taekwondo Academy. We entered the dojang. It was small, and the rooms had tables in the middle of them not conducive to martial art's practice. There was one small, cluttered office off to one side where we found Master Choi dressed in plain clothes. Master Choi walked out to greet us. He smiled, shook our hands, and seemed happy to see us. His dojang doubled as a teaching center that's why there were tables in the center. Master Choi was a tutor and used the space during the day for education and taught taekwondo in the evenings. We spoke briefly of our intentions. Our meeting lasted about fifteen minutes, and then we headed home unclear of what had just happened. We had asked if he'd still be interested in teaching us again and advancing us when it was time but Master Choi just had sat and listened. He never answered. His only comment was, "Oh, you have lots of material, too much," when we showed him the thick binder containing all the things we had learned over the years. Our conversation in the car on the way home was one of dismay and confusion. Was he willing to help or not? We were unsure but didn't know anyone else. A few days later, Master Choi called and invited us to his school. It was strange that he asked us to return to his school when we knew he only lived about three miles from my father's house, but he asked us to drive the hour again to Loudonville. We drove down, uniforms and gear in hand, wondering what he might ask us to perform or how he would deem us worthy of his teachings again. We again just sat and talked. Master Choi picked up the phone and called Korea while we sat. He laughed and joked with the person on the other end he claimed to be his childhood friend at the Kukkiwon. He spoke in Korean so we had no idea what was said. Our second meeting ended in a similar way. We walked away, unclear if he was willing to help. We questioned if this was just a test of our loyalty and dedication to him. We could have had these meetings in our town or at our house. We didn't need to be driving all that distance for such a short conversation. Three times, we traveled down to his school in Loudonville before he finally took out as small piece of paper and wrote down on the paper a couple poomsae and a few other things that he requested my father learn. Next, he wrote down two names: Munger and Lee. He told my father once he knew everything on the piece of paper, he was to contact these men. They lived in Pennsylvania. Talking to Master Choi was challenging with his poor English, but he was a man of few words, which made it even harder. We weren't entirely sure what this meant but figured it was part of him testing our loyalty again. I figured this was my opportunity to ask about learning hapkido from him since I remember he used to teach it to a few students back in our early days. He sat and thought for a minute, surprised I asked. He took out a book and a couple dusty videos and said, "You buy, learn, and maybe I call." A quick glimpse of the materials he showed me was that of a beginner. He was asking to learn things he taught to beginners years ago. My father and I again drove home confused again.

My father spent weeks learning and practicing the items requested by Master Choi. I helped him practice and get ready. He made the call to Lee and Munger and set up a time to visit them. He wasn't sure what else would be requested of him. He knew over forty poomsae from previous years' studies, including more than a dozen black belt poomsae. He had no idea what they would ask of him and was prepared to show all if needed. He only had a few items on a piece of paper and wasn't sure what else would be required of him. He headed by car by himself to Pennsylvania. It had started to snow on his way down, which made for a slippery drive. He had more than a four-hour drive ahead of him. He arrived at a plaza and met Munger and Lee for the first time. Both were taekwondo grand masters and ran a school together in a basement of a plaza. The sign-out front said "Karate," so my father had trouble finding it. When asked about why it didn't say taekwondo they replied, "Taekwondo too big." The small staircase entrance in the plaza was too small to fit the word taekwondo, so they shortened the sign to simply read Karate.

My father was asked to perform all his materials in front of these two total strangers. He performed everything asked of him very well and expected they'd continue and want to see more. He was prepared and eager to perform after all his hard work and preparation. The test not only consisted of performing poomsae in front of the two of them but also consisted of a battery of questions. They questioned him regarding how he saw the future of taekwondo as a sport and how it related to the future of my father's teachings. They asked his opinion of the influence of mixed martial on taekwondo and the Olympics. They were digging into his inner workings and what type of taekwondo he intended to spread. After years of studying under different instructors we realized that the way we intended to spread was much more important than any new move we might ever learn. He was there a couple of hours alone, doing everything asked of him and answering all questions, wondering what would be next. The storm had gotten bad, so Grand Masters Munger and Lee decided to cut things short. They asked him to drive home and record a video of the board break he was asked to perform. They also requested he videotape the poomsae that Master Choi had requested as well. Once completed they asked the videos be returned to Master Choi. My father made the trek home on snow-covered roads, not fully knowing the purpose of this journey.

I hadn't received any response from Master Choi about hapkido, so I decided to explore other avenues. I made over a dozen phone calls and sent numerous emails, all of which led to dead ends. Determined to continue and ensure we could offer more than just taekwondo, I persisted. Finally, I got a message back. I was asked to reach out to the director of hapkido for this particular group, and he'd talk to me more about it. The phone call was fruitful, and I set up a meeting. I drove two hours by car downstate, prepared to show my skills. My father and I drove to meet a man and determine if he'd be willing to continue to teach me hapkido. We were greeted warmly as we arrived, but I could sense some skepticism. I was asked to perform to validate my abilities and credentials. I performed everything he requested and felt competent in all my abilities. The gentleman seemed impressed and offered a relationship with him and the hapkido organization he belonged. He was willing to help as long as I followed their curriculum and guidelines. I was thrilled and couldn't wait to get started. My father was right there by my side, just as excited as I was. We could now add hapkido to the schedule at the new school.

Murray's Family Martial Arts Center quickly began to prosper. He had many students who came to attend from the previous school. There were more than forty students, mostly families, that decided to follow him. He quickly became the largest martial arts school in the area. The family name had become very well known in the area as a result of his excellent reputation in taekwondo. He treated me like his partner. He always valued my opinions and suggestions more than his own. Regardless of the rank he wore, he always had the utmost respect for me in the dojang. He was the higher rank but you could never tell because he had more respect for me than anyone else in the school. I've worked with lots of higher ranks who would never take criticism or instruction from anyone lower, but this never happened to my father. He remained humble and open to every one of my suggestions inside or outside of the dojang. He embraced every opportunity and forged into every challenge like a true warrior. He took every opportunity to put me on a pedestal in front of the students and accredit me with the accomplishments of the school; he was an example of humility.

My father made his dream a reality and business was better than ever. Two of the smaller taekwondo schools in the area had closed down. They both seemed to be struggling when I had previously checked them out anyways. My father taught three classes a day for five days each week and then two classes on Saturdays. He had a few black belt instructors who assisted, but he taught ever class himself. He ran all the colored belt testing himself, and then when he had someone ready for a black belt, he would schedule it so I could be present and offer input. He really valued my opinions on each student. I could be more objective and offer different criticisms since I did not see these students as regular as he did. I taught my three hapkido classes each week. Most of Mr. Donahue's hapkido students decided to follow me when they heard I started the hapkido program at the new school. Then, I tried to pop in for a couple late taekwondo classes to help my father when I didn't have to work.

My father became well known for all the ways he personally went into the community and promoted his business. The most famous was his charity board-breaking events and fundraisers. He and his students helped raise money for individuals in need in the community. He would hand-cut thousands of boards for breaking. All students would go out in the community to help raise money. This was something he loved to do each year, and he made it into a huge production. The donations the students collected allowed them to participate in this enormous board-break event. There were food sales. There were hairdressers, including both my sisters, on the premises donating their time and trade to promote the events. My sisters both donated all their earnings to the event. There were martial arts demonstrations, and everyone got involved. Local news stations and newspapers would often report on the events. It was the single biggest event of the year. Each student looked forward to it year after year. He and the students would break thousands of boards and donate all the proceeds to charity. He made the community come together for his events.

"Murray's Family Martial Center annual charity board break event and Fundraiser"

My father also conducted numerous martial arts demonstrations several times per year. He could be seen at the local fairs, carnivals, and garage sale events. He loved to be able to bring his students anywhere to show off their skills. He brought his students to events held at the local college and could often be seen performing in the nearby parks. He hosted ladies self-defense seminars several times a year. He became known for the ladies' self-defense clinics he offered

47

and how he used them to empower and educate women all across the area. He taught self defense at many of the area schools for children. He was invited back each year by area schools to work with their young people. He was invited to teach defensive tactics to criminal justice students so they may strengthen their skills. He even taught a few classes with a few local police officers seeking additional hand-to-hand combat. He truly loved teaching and sharing his knowledge. He offered all these services and events at no charge. I helped whenever possible but he did most of this work himself. He spread his name and his love of taekwondo throughout the community.

Both of my sisters had their children enrolled in taekwondo. A couple of the children had become black belts and also assisted in instruction on occasion. My younger sister also wanted to be involved in the school again. She had been a black belt in taekwondo when we were younger but hadn't done taekwondo since. She wanted to offer and be able to run her own new program. She was always a fitness buff and eager to learn any new fitness fad possible. She had been a powerlifter. She had done CrossFit. She had become a certified personal trainer herself and loved to teach and motivate others. So, my sister decided to add cardio kickboxing classes to the current schedule. She went out and learned all the routines and became certified as a cardio kickboxing instructor. Eager to begin, she started some classes and quickly filled the room. My father bought additional equipment to support the program, and it quickly became a success. Now, Murray's Family Martial Arts center offered taekwondo, hapkido, and cardio kickboxing.

The school had become a success! It was no surprise with all the hard work and time my father dedicated. He had created something bigger and better than ever before. The students loved it and continued to come from his ex-partner's school. My father always had a soft spot in his heart, particularly for those that struggled. He never turned anyone away. He believed everyone deserved a chance to learn from taekwondo. He believed that anyone could do it if just given an opportunity and the right guidance. He had students in wheel chairs. He had hearing-impaired students. He had many students with attention deficit disorder, attention deficit hyper activity disorder, students with autism, and many other learning disabilities He treated them the same and they all learned. Everyone was required to complete the same requirements as the other students but he gave more help to anyone that may need it. One day, this young lady in her late teens entered through the door. My father greeted her as he would any prospective student. She proceeded to tell him that she was sent over from Upstate Taekwondo and Hapkido. My father was surprised that he would willingly send over any students. He asked her why she was sent over to him. She replied, "Mr. Donahue said I'd fit in better here." This young lady had an obvious learning disability, and they didn't want her because she didn't learn as quickly and easily as other students. My father strapped on a belt and threw her right into class with everyone else. She had no natural ability and noticeable physical limitations, but she worked hard and tried. My father was courteous to all. He could remember his own struggles and his ability to overcome and preserve. He was confident he could make that happen with anyone. He felt it was his responsibility to stand up for those who were weaker and couldn't stand up for themselves. Everyone in his classes had fun and learned. All of his instructors were just like him and spent a little extra time with those that needed it.

We were ready to attend our first tournament together as a school. One of the instructors dedicated time to student development. He went off to become a certified coach to properly train all the students. The students dedicated countless hours to sharpening their skills for the big day. My father purchased matching jackets for a group to stand out at the event. All were ready to attend and compete. Just prior to attending, my father received a letter. The letter stated that he and his students were not welcome to attend this tournament. Mr. Donahue had conspired with the directors at the tournament and convinced them to prevent our school from attending. My father and I were shocked. We didn't know what to tell the students after all their hard work. They would surely be disappointed. We would have to seek other tournaments for our students to be able to attend.

My father's trip to Pennsylvania proved to be productive. Master Choi showed up one day with a certificate from Korea for my father. He not only promoted my father to his next rank which was grand master in taekwondo, but sanctioned his school as a Kukkiwon certification center. He would be able to process paperwork through this direct channel that Master Choi had set up for him. He also went through the extra trouble of registering my father with his childhood Kwan. This was a prestigious honor for my father and the school. This linked us to Master Choi's Taekwondo origins and meant he wanted my father and I to carry forward the art as it was originally intended. We were in a good position to be able to continue to help all our students and black belts as the progressed.

My father being honored as Grand Master in Taekwondo by Master Choi.

One day my father stopped by to visit me at work. He asked me to go outside and talk to him, which was unusual. He proceeded to tell me as we stood together in the parking lot that he had cancer. I wasn't sure how to react. I just stood there. He said that he explored all his options, and radiation was his best treatment option. He and my mother had decided that would be best for him. I continued to just stand there not knowing what to say or do. He seemed really upbeat and positive. He didn't seem sad at all. I never knew the words to say, so I said nothing until he started to leave, and I told him I loved him. I really didn't know what this meant or how it would affect things. He started treatments shortly after our conversation that day.

My father didn't let cancer stop him or slow him down. He was active in the community promoting his business and actively teaching almost twenty classes a week. I encouraged my father to start hapkido, and he said, "well, maybe." He eventually joined. He didn't seem to enjoy it like taekwondo. I could tell he did it for me because I asked. I could tell he wasn't excited about it like me. He strapped on a white belt and began to learn. It reminded me of the old days in the garage. He worked side by side with all his other students. He was the grand master now wearing a white belt in his own school. He was so humble and never asked or expected special treatment. He wanted to learn everything just like a newcomer. He did this for three years and eventually earned his black belt in hapkido, too.

Master Choi presenting letter of accommodation to Murray's Family Martial Arts.

Meanwhile, I focused more of my attention on hapkido. I was asked to attend a hapkido seminar downstate. I had encouraged my father and our other students to attend to broaden everyone's knowledge base. My father was not thrilled to be going to the seminar, but he went anyways. We had a blast once we got there and learned a lot. We were also able to make several contacts in the martial arts community. The next time an opportunity came up to attend a seminar, my father and the other students were eager to attend. We attended a couple seminars a year until one year, I was asked to host a seminar upstate in our small town. Without hesitation, I agreed. I never took a minute to ask my father if this was okay or if the school could afford such an undertaking. My father would have to do most of the work. He would make the calls to find a venue. He would have to promote through direct mail, emails, and social media. He would handle the registration fees and track the participants. He would need to set up hotel reservations and dinner reservations for our guests of honor. He did all this with no complaints. He embraced the idea of hosting such a big undertaking. The event was a success and turned out to be one of the largest hapkido events ever held in the northeast. He agreed to host another a year later.

"Picture from Combat Hapkido seminar hosted by Murray's Family Martial Arts Center in 2011"

My father constantly sought ways to broaden his knowledge, continue his training, and provide his instructors and students with the best education possible. He regularly invited guest instructors and grand masters to inspire and educate his students. I rode his coattails along for the ride. I tried to stay behind the scenes as much as possible but always supported him every step of the way. He also liked to make me the center of attention and gave me credit whenever the opportunity was to arise, but it was really him who made the business a success. He was now a grand master in taekwondo. He was a black belt in hapkido. What was next? He paid to have an instructor come to the school to teach and certify us in tai chi. He went off with one of his students to get certified in an anatomical pressure point curriculum. He attended seminars to learn ground survival. He studied videos and learned from experts on additional weapons disarmament. He always went off and took the opportunity to learn something new, not for him, but so he could bring it back to share with me and all his other students. He lived, slept, and breathed taekwondo and had devoted most of his adult life to the art and improvement of others.

My father wanted me to take over the school and constantly would ask. I never seriously considered it because, as successful as it was, it would not allow me to quit my day job. The day job paid the bills and provided a lifestyle. For me, martial arts was still a hobby. I would love to have it be my side business and additional source of income, but my work schedule wouldn't allow me to be there any more than I already was. My father had several instructors, but they were unpaid and not always dependable. He was retired and able to be there whenever anyone else couldn't. I didn't see a way to make it work. I loved riding the wave and enjoying the martial arts lifestyle without the commitment or obligations that he had.

We traveled to seminars and ceremonies together across the country and loved having the opportunity to learn and grow as a team. My father was nominated for several awards, including inductions to a hall of fame at several different times, but politely declined. He was spreading a seed. He didn't do it for him. He did it for all his students. He was not looking for any recognition. He did it purely for the love of his students.

My father let me lead the way whenever I wanted. He forged forward, creating the dream we had always discussed as colored belts, Murray's Taekwondo and Pizza to Go.

Chapter Six - Bonds & Friendships

The Koreans have an emotion referred to as Jeong [1] that expresses the closeness we feel in our relationships. It is an emotion influenced by our beliefs and our past. It's the emotion that develops the bonds we share with other individuals through our experiences. It's a complex emotion but describes the bonds my father and I felt with so many people throughout our martial arts journey. We created these bonds with our instructors, students, and taekwondo peers. These bonds were developed through our experiences in taekwondo over time without us realizing it.

Mr. and Mrs. Hammond were the trailblazers in the web of martial arts connections we forged. Twice a week for several years, they graciously opened their home to all their students. They taught in their basement for several years, right up until I was seventeen and headed to college. We all shared our personal lives with each other in their basement. We learned from the successes and failures of them and our fellow students along the road to our black belts. We all became close friends and would stay in touch years after the Hammonds closed their school. We were especially grateful to the Hammonds for getting us started and teaching us what the art really meant. They served to be part-time teachers, psychologists, mentors, coaches, as well as friends. They helped me through struggles in gym class or other sports by addressing my concerns in class. They would spend time practicing skills unrelated to taekwondo so that I may improve in after-school sports or gym classes. They didn't have to but they chose that helping just one individual who may be struggling was more important than that day's lesson of kicking and punching. They were there to listen when one of us had a bad day. They offered support and guidance for the struggles we had outside of the dojang. We often arrived to class thirty to forty minutes early to class to stretch. Stretching meant talking out the day's struggles and learning from each other how to navigate them. All of their students took advantage of this time as the pre-class time served as invaluable in our life's journey. Most of their students were co-workers, friends, or referrals. They didn't advertise or promote their business other than word of mouth. Stretching before class seemed like a social hour sometimes, but it turned out to be a safe space

---

[1] Jee, L.H. (2002). Hanmaeum, One Heart-One mind: A Korean Buddhist Philosophical Basis of Jeong.
In: Chung, E.Y..J., Oh, J.S. (eds) Emotions in Korean Philosophy and Religion.
Palgrave Studios Comparative East-West Philosophy.
Palgrave Macmillan, Cham.
Https://doi.org/10.1007/978-3-030-94747_9

for all of us. Discussions of the day's going on and what is happening in our world provided us with our own little support group. All of our fellow students and our instructors would actively participate in similar discussions, so we began to know everyone in class on a personal level. Since I didn't have many friends when I was younger, my fellow students became my friends and I looked forward each week to our discussions and becoming closer. When one of us had trouble in school, they focused on that night's lesson to relate and help them through it. When someone had a conflict at work, they addressed it. If one of us brought up a real-life self-defense scenario, we took class time to work out a solution. They cared about each student's success. We built friendships with members of our small group. Mr. Hammond and a fellow student, Charlie Harris, both worked for the same company as my father. They all knew each other and had much in common at work to talk about. Mr. Harris practiced together with his son at the Hammond's school. My father and I looked up to and admired both Mr. Harris and his son as higher ranks but also as another father/son team sharing an activity together. Mrs. Hammond even offered me my first job as a teenager for the auction house she ran. We were really like one big family who shared and cared and came together a couple times a week. The Hammonds also threw taekwondo parties where we all got together and did activities like volleyball or kickball as a group outside of taekwondo. The Hammonds were invited and attended major events in our lives. Even many years after they closed their school and no longer practiced martial arts, they made a point to attend my father's grand opening event when he opened his solo school to encourage him on his journey.

Being two of Choi's highest-ranking students, the Hammonds, at that time, seemed to have a similar bond with Master Choi as we did with them. They always did as he said inside and outside of the dojang. We strived to share in this relationship with him too. One day, Mr. Hammond told us Master Choi asked us to show up on a Sunday. We were so excited! We thought this meant we were to learn something exclusive from him. We hoped it'd be a private or semi-private lesson from Master Choi himself. Not knowing what it was, we all showed up, bags in hand. We arrived to discover Master Choi needed our help moving the carpeting and equipment because he was moving his dojang to a new location. We stuffed as many items as we could into our cars and began to transport his equipment to the new location. As a result of these non-teaching hours, we became closer to Master Choi than other students. He was our instructor, and that was clear. He displayed professionalism in class and at the dojang. There was no partiality, but there was definitely a strong bond and understanding he created with his instructors, those who dedicated their lives to furthering the art. We looked up to Master Choi for the rank and position he held as our instructor, and grand master but also for the pioneer he was bringing taekwondo across the water to spread Korean national support to America. A man who traveled half way across the world to start a small school in an upstate rural area where taekwondo was not yet known. He had to overcome a language barrier as well as be able to support himself in this new land. He taught Mathematics during the day to provide for his family but honored his country by spreading their national sport years before it became popular in the Olympics.

A couple years after the Hammonds had closed their school, Master Choi again asked us for help on a Sunday. This time, he had asked us to come to his house. We were so surprised he invited us to his home. He had asked only a select few of us, so this made us feel special. We had become close to him from his teachings and were always available any time he asked us for extra help. So this must be it! We finally were going to receive a special course or instruction that he only shares with a select few. We thought maybe it would be acupuncture or an internal healing lesson since we were told he practiced those, too. We piled in the car with only two other students and headed to his house. What a privilege and honor to be invited to our grand master's house. We again showed up, bags in hand, again expecting some special lesson. Once there, he opened the door and, standing in plain clothes, he smiled and greeted us. He asked us to come right in. We slowly moved inside as he points upstairs to this giant grand piano. In his broken English, he asked us to help him move it downstairs. I thought this was surely not the lesson but maybe a test? I saw *Karate Kid* several times there must be a lesson somewhere here. No, it was simply because he needed some able-bodied individuals as grunt labor. Maybe it wasn't the lesson I had expected, but it was nice to be able to help, and it made us feel special that he asked us over anyone else. In those days, we never seemed to be as close to Master Choi as he was with the Hammonds. This may be because he had many more students to share his teaching with but he certainly made us stand apart from the other students at times like these. We felt a special connection to him as he did with us. A connection that later drew us back to him years later.

Master Choi often developed a connection with many of his high-ranking black belts. The years of close personal interaction and dedication to the art made them different than the thousands of students who joined and never stuck with the art. He had trust in certain ones more than others. Mr. Mulches, although he didn't practice in town any longer, definitely stood out. He used his taekwondo knowledge to make a career that few people ever accomplished. But Master Choi trusted Mr. Mulches like no one else I ever saw. To be able to trust an individual enough to let them hammer down on you in the midst of a room full of spectators without causing damage requires an immense amount of trust. I can't image that's a demonstration you practice over and over, or at all. So to know and understand that person that well describes their friendship especially considering he hadn't seen or practiced with Mr. Mulches for years prior. He only trusted Mr. Mulches to do things like this with him. As a result, when Mr. Mulches was no longer able to return, Master Choi never again performed demonstrations like he did with him.

During our early days with Choi's Taekwondo Academy we made many taekwondo friends and learned so many valuable lessons to start our journey. A notable pair, Bob and Brenda Locke, exemplified this camaraderie. Both surpassing my father and me in rank, they were formidable black belts. Occasionally, they lent their expertise at Choi's in guiding class instruction. Mr Locke loved sparring. He liked to be rough and tough and could hold his own against the younger teenagers. He was mostly hands when he sparred like my father. They both worked at area mills, so they often had union stories to share and compare. Mrs. Locke was the resident poomsae expert. She practiced them continually before and after class. When anyone had a question about a poomsae, she was the one everyone went to learn. She willingly helped Master Choi's students even though everyone could tell she would rather be aside practicing independently. They had a daughter who was the same age as my sister, so there were always lots of life stories we as a family shared. Mr. Locke was 5 foot seven inches tall and stocky build. He claimed to be over 350 pounds at one time before he joined taekwondo. He had a large amount of excess belly skin that was noticeable in the locker rooms from his excessive weight loss. He spent his time before class jumping rope. He claimed it was part of what kept him in shape, and he didn't want to return to that higher weight. I hated jumping rope but enjoyed watching him perform it with ease and seamlessly like a pro boxer. Since I was terrible at it, I avoided jumping rope and stuck to practicing kicks and poomsae. Mr. Locke would always encourage me to join, but being slightly chubby myself I hated the idea of everything bouncing up and down and couldn't manage to get a rhythm. I tried it with him a few times and just gave up. I would leave it to the experts.

One day, we walked into the dojang and noticed a new test requirement board affixed to the wall. Each level had a designated number of jump rope requirements in addition to our basic movements, poomsae, sparring, and breaking requirements. I became angered. I was only a few months away from my second degree black belt exam and now had to master a skill I could barley perform. The requirements started off very modest for colored belts. Twenty single jumps at yellow, forty at green belt, and so on. At blue belt level, the single jumps requirement was sixty and then blue belts were required to be able to do double jump ropes as well. The chart increased with every belt level. As someone testing for a second-degree black belt at that time, I was required to be able to perform one thousand singles and fifty doubles. I was infuriated. Why would Master Choi suddenly add such requirements so close to test day? I was sure Mr. Locke had something to do with this. I was convinced he was setting me up to fail. I had enough to worry about for test day. Now, I had the added stress of attempting a skill that I knew I was terrible at. There was only one thing to do. I went directly to Mr. Locke and asked for help. He recommended I buy a nice quality jump rope and dedicate fifteen minutes a day to jump roping. That sounded easy but there was no way only fifteen minutes was going to make me jump rope like Mr. Locke. The next day I went out and bought a heavy leather jump rope just like he used. I was not alone. The whole place turned into a jump rope training center. Every single student had seen the notice and all were concerned and decided to devote time before class to hitting these new requirements.

I was terrible. I couldn't string together more than three or four singles without missing. I was ready to give up already. The colored belts had requirements that seemed achievable with a little work, but I wouldn't be able to get to a thousand in time. Besides, I hadn't even attempted a double; I was too uncoordinated to make that happen. I went back to Mr. Locke with my head down. "I just don't know how to do this. Can you help me? What am I doing wrong?" I said.

He was jumping, roping and in a deep sweat. He replied, "You just have to do it. Dedicate fifteen minutes a day to it every day, and if you miss, start over until your fifteen minutes is up." He made it sound so simple. This statement just annoyed me more. I went and found a corner to finish out my fifteen minutes with no improvement. I tried this every day at the dojang before class. I decided I needed more time at home where I didn't look like such a fool in front of the others. A couple weeks went by, and many of the students were managing to find a rhythm and performing well, except me. I had managed to string along 15-20 at a time but not consistently. I hadn't figured out the timing on a double yet either. I noticed that once I got frustrated, I couldn't manage to string together more than one or two, but when I was relaxed, I might hit twenty. I was so discouraged looking around and seeing everyone else getting better while I was not. I would watch Mr. Locke jump rope for the entire time he was there before class without missing a beat, sometimes that would be forty to fifty minutes straight.

I continued my fifteen minutes before class and attempted to spend thirty minutes or more at home because I needed to make headway fast. After consistent dedication, a few weeks later, I could string along more than fifty singles, and I got my first double ever. I was so excited! I couldn't wait to tell Mr. Locke. He, while jump roping, said, "Thats' great. Now try to incorporate one double into your singles for a while until you can get two." I did exactly as he said and finally started to see small improvements. Although, all this jump roping was aggravating my calves. They were sore and swollen, and the pain kept me from being able to practice every day. I had to slow down and only jump rope the days I went to class. The additional days at home were too much. So, I increased my time from fifteen minutes before class to thirty. If I couldn't do it every day because of the pain, I would just have to do more time on the other days. I started to notice in sessions that I jump roped longer than fifteen minutes, and my breathing became a limiter. I could now do more than 100 singles and 5 doubles but I would get so out of breath I'd have to take five minutes or more to recover. I was getting better but still had a long way to go.

I asked Mr. Locke, "Am I required to do all those singles and doubles without missing like you?" I had gotten better but was not confident I'd hit the mark and be able to be a pro like Mr. Locke.

He replied, "Yes," as he continued jumping rope. I wasn't sure that was possible for me. It seemed like another setback. I had gotten better but my calves and breathing were not ever going to hold out for 1000 singles and fifty doubles.

I increased my practice sessions to 40-50 minutes before class, like Mr. Locke and continued to see improvements. I could do more than five hundred singles and now could do more than ten doubles without missing. I felt accomplished, but my test was less than two months away. I was determined to not look like a fool in front of the others. I wanted to perform like a black belt and needed to find a way to make this happen. I felt it was becoming achievable. I continued my practices before every class until about a week before my test. I could now do a thousand singles without missing and hit fifty doubles. I was ready! I had overcome my inadequacies and accomplished the given task. On the day of my test, I arrived early. I was there before everyone, including the Lockes. I got dressed and started practicing. I saw Mr. Locke enter with his bag in hand, and he walked over to the jump rope requirement sheet attached to the wall. He looked at me with a grin as he reached up and tore the page off the wall. He crumpled it up and threw it in the trash as he entered the changing room. I was angry but realized, in that moment, he had done it all for me. He had done it to help me realize it was possible. Master Choi never asked anyone to jump rope that day. He knew of Mr. Locke's intentions but never tried to stop it or tell anyone it wouldn't actually be required.

I learned a lot about myself that day. I learned that I truly could accomplish anything I put my mind to, and I had Mr. Locke to thank for that. He could be gruff sometimes and seemed self-absorbed at times, but he cared enough about me and my well-being to teach me an invaluable lesson that would stick with me forever. He saw the drive and determination in me to be able to accomplish feats I saw as impossible. He had a whole class focused on a fictitious requirement just because I was in awe over his jump roping abilities and thought I couldn't achieve that myself.

My father liked working with Mrs. Locke. He never enjoyed poomsae but saw them as a necessary part of his progression, but it wasn't fun like sparring. To both of us, poomsae was simply a way to learn more skills for sparring. My father loved to watch Mrs. Locke practice her poomsae. She had confidence and grace while performing. She was a tall woman with extremely high kicks and made the poomsae look easy. My father would follow her in her movements whenever given the opportunity. He wanted to be able to perform them like she did. She took him under her wing and offered pointers and constructive criticisms. They would spend time before each class practicing together. My father, because of Mrs. Locke, started to appreciate the poomsae in a way he hadn't ever before. They became more than a belt requirement. They became an expression of himself and his abilities. They became a way to actively meditate and work on his inner self. Poomsae would forever take on a new meaning and purpose as a result of the time Mrs. Locke dedicated to him.

There were many students who had followed my father from the previous location. They felt a special connection with him as their instructor but as a person too. He brought these students in close and watched them grow as individuals and as martial artists. Entire families, drawn by his mentorship, left their former school to reunite with my father once more. They practiced together as a family because they loved my father and his way. Working closely with an individual or family so closely for years in an effort to help them achieve their goals and dreams provides a closeness with that instructor that is carried on long after their training ends. They not only looked up to and admired him as an instructor, but they all confided in him and trusted him with personal matters. My father treated everyone like his own family. He did so much so that he had to put the family in the business's name. I first thought he devised the name because we were a family of martial artists with he and I doing it together, and then my sister, and then our children. But the family referred to his extended martial arts family. It was the community that he built through taekwondo. He understood this so much earlier than I did. His method of encouraging families to practice together was not only because of how he got started but was because he saw the value it could provide within the family structure itself. It was a way for families to bond through the martial arts. It was an opportunity for them to come together for a greater purpose. He believed this so much he created a slogan for his shirt and advertisements, "where families get their kicks." He would spread the tenets of taekwondo: courtesy, integrity, perseverance, self-control, and indomitable spirit throughout the family structure. Families brought him troubled teens. They brought him kids with disabilities. Often, students came to my father seeking what was lacking in their family's everyday balance. They wanted structure and discipline. They were seeking a set a values they could teach to their children and would carry through to their homes. In a world that lacks morals and ethics, my father created a set of core values for these families to live by and guide their families. That's why so many families followed him and looked up to him. He had the integrity to stand up for what he believed taekwondo did for the community. He had the indomitable spirit within him to make it happen. They needed his guidance in their lives and learned to use it to guide their families through life's obstacles.

One particular woman started with a self-defense class with my father when he was still with Mr. Donahue. She was so impressed with the class that she decided to join taekwondo to learn more. This particular student took a liking to my father because of his real-world approach to self-defense. She signed up and eventually earned her black belt under my father and Mr. Donahue. She continued to become more involved with the school and looked forward to the opportunity to participate in future self-defense clinics using her newly acquired skills. She saw the importance of these events and encouraged all participants to join, too like she had. She would recruit personal friends and coworkers to attend these clinics, seeing the value in what taekwondo was promoting. When my father left and opened his own school, she was one of the first to call and say, "I'm coming. I'll follow you wherever you go." She became an instructor at the new school. She went on to lead ladies self defense clinics. She became a family friend, offering feedback and advise. She volunteered to help in whatever capacity she could. She loved teaching but loved most spreading the Murray's way. She shared in my father's new found love for poomsae, and she became the resident poomsae expert and addressed all related questions. She felt an allegiance to my father like no other and became a permanent fixture at the school.

One family that attended was a father with two children who all did taekwondo together. All earned black belts together. They originally started together in taekwondo with my father and Mr. Donahue. The father and his two children went over to the new school shortly after opening. His wife wanted to be involved, too, so she started a not-for-profit organization to benefit the students of Murray's Family Martial Arts Center. They raised money to cover tournament expenses and gave gifts to testing candidates. The whole family showed up for every board break fundraiser charity event, every black belt exam, and every demonstration on or off the premises. He also became an active instructor for the school, teaching classes when my father couldn't be there. He earned a black belt in hapkido while with Murray's Family Martial Arts Center and helped teach hapkido classes as well. He also attended every training seminar and never missed an event. He and my father drove thirteen hours in a car one day together to attend an anatomical targeting certification class. My father covered the expenses because it meant so much to him to have such a dedicated student. My father treated him like family. Our families had grown up together and went to the same high school. We were close growing up in a small town.

My father had more than twenty families ranging in size from two to seven family members, all practicing together at once. My father's school was filled with families like this who trained and bonded together. My father treated them like family and became their mentor, psychologist, teacher, and friend, much like Mr. and Mrs. Hammond had done for us. His school had individuals too, but most started as one, and eventually, my father would encourage other family members to join as well. If they didn't have other family members to bring, he would get them to bring distant relatives or friends. One led to more as he continued to build the empire.

When Master Choi sent my father to Pennsylvania for his next belt test, we initially thought it was a test of his will and determination. We couldn't understand why Master Choi didn't conduct the test himself, considering his ninth-degree mastery in taekwondo. He certainly could have, but he chose not to. He could have certainly made things easy by conducting a small black belt test here without the need to travel four hours in a car in the middle of a snowstorm, but he didn't. There was more. Master Choi asked my father and me to return to Pennsylvania later to assist Grand Masters Lee and Munger. He asked us to return with ideas to help promote and market their business. We sat with the two of them causally and spoke of strategies to increase their Facebook and website presence. We were asked to share ways we used to successfully market Murray's Family Martial Arts Center. We did this because Master Choi asked it of us, expecting nothing in return. What we didn't realize until later Master Choi was creating a bond for us with his lineage. Lee and Munger were not only other high-ranking grandmasters in taekwondo but they were from the direct lineage of Master Choi's childhood Kwan. Master Choi wanted to insure a connection in the event one day he was not able to assist us. He wanted us to know where to reach out and who we could trust to carry on the art the way he intended it to be passed on.

Over this martial arts journey I started to realize the bonds I had created with my fellow students was something notable and something I didn't see in other areas of my life. I had few friends growing up, and none I valued or trusted. Coworkers from my jobs were simply colleagues. Rarely would I ever spend time with a coworker out together and never identified them as friends. Individuals outside the martial arts community often lacked the same values as those I surrounded myself with my whole life. I struggled to identify or relate on a personal level to those who didn't share in the moral code I learned to identify with through taekwondo.

One lesson I learned from my father early in life was that friends will come and go, but family is forever. He went on further to explain that the only people we can truly count on are also family. His lesson proved true countless times in my life. He did extend this to our martial arts family. There were so many students and instructors that he brought close to him and treated him like family. These martial arts bonds have lasted over time. I'm not referring to those who try taekwondo or do it for a few months. I'm referring to those who let it become a part of them. There's a certain type of person who sticks around and commits to martial arts as a lifestyle. This doesn't mean that everyone who takes a martial arts class or students for a year or two has an unbreakable bond with their instructors and fellow students, but the few who choose to make it a lifestyle have some characteristics different than others. I'm not sure if they find the art or if the art finds them, but something internally makes it a choice of how to live their life.

When we first approached Master Choi to assist us with the new school, we questioned Master Choi's willingness at first. After all, it had been many years without contact and we popped into his life again because we needed his help. I'm not sure I would have been as accepting and willing to help. I definitely would have been extremely skeptical and cautious as he was. His decision to help stemmed from that bond created so many years earlier. This bond stayed in tack and developed into a great friendship later in life. After my father started his school, Master Choi and my father went out for coffee together regularly. They talked about martial arts and business, but more importantly, they talked about life. Two men in their late sixties, they had a lot in common and tons to talk about that wasn't taekwondo.

One day, Master Choi opened up to my father over coffee. He said, "Oh Bobby, I sorry 'bout Greggy. I not know he like that." Naturally my father assumed the conversation was in reference to how my father and Mr. Donahue's business relationship ended. He proceeded, "He tell me close school, or he open cross street." He continued, "Greggy crazy; he once ask me I know how to kill someone." He sipped his coffee. "I afraid and not know what he try to do," so I leave school to him and move away." He had threatened and pushed Choi out. My father was shocked to hear this and didn't know any of this had transpired. Master Choi continued, "Bobby, I should have given school to you. I sorry." My father was in awe and didn't know what to say. So many years later, after being partners with Mr. Donahue for 10 years, to find out now. They finished their coffee. My father was flabbergasted and couldn't believe his ears.

In another coffee visit with Master Choi a couple years later. He learned the reason that Master Choi was never recognized as head of the AAU tournament years earlier. Apparently, Mr. Donahue had arrived at the tournament earlier that day to meet with a group of high-ranking Americans, part of this new wave of taekwondo spreading across the United States. Mr. Donahue had already become friends with the members of this group with intentions of taking over Master Choi's school. He had met with them before the tournament that day to discuss a Korean taking over as head of an American athletic organization like the AAU. Mr. Donahue strongly expressed his concerns to the American board and convinced them that this was not a good idea. He felt it should be awarded to an American, not a Korean. Master Choi had been sabotaged behind his back. The board decided to award the position to an American on the day of the event.

Seeing the obstacles Master Choi had to overcome and the hand Mr. Donahue had played in it all, explained the skepticism Master Choi had the day we showed up seeking his help. I am surprised, looking back that he decided to help at all. I believe it was due to his love of taekwondo and his desire to continue to spread his art. He saw something different in my father. He saw someone who also shared his passion for doing good in the community. He saw someone who would spread the art as he intended.

The school was prospering, and my father had created a martial arts empire. He was well known in the community and had a team of instructors in taekwondo, hapkido, tai chi, cardio-kickboxing, and self-defense. He was living the martial arts dream we had spoke of when we first started. Master Choi and my father were set to meet for coffee again, so I asked to tag along. Master Choi was smiling and excited to hear of the success. He never asked for any financial compensation or to be part of the business. He was genuinely happy for my father's success. He looked up from his coffee and said, "Bobby, you be the pebble. We throw you pebble into the water; you students be the ripples." A man of few words had spoken and told the story of his life and legacy, and how my father and I played a part in it as well.

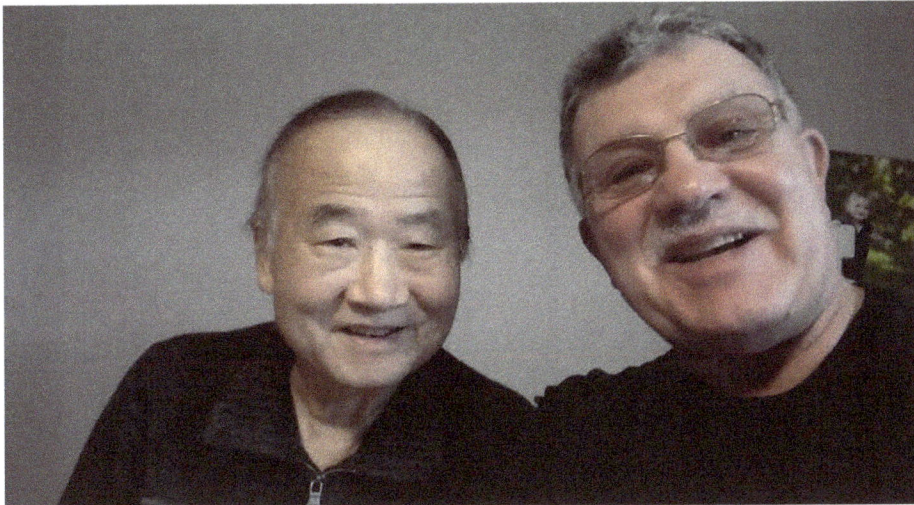

"My father at coffee with Master Choi."

Master Choi never saw teaching and empowering his students as a competition. He brought taekwondo to the United States with the hopes of spreading tang soo do [2] (the name for

---

[2] Michael A. Demarco, MA.
Taekwondo, The Korean Martial Art,
Via Media Publishing Company

taekwondo when he first learned it) culture. He was not threatened by someone wanting to progress and open a school elsewhere. He allowed Mr. Terry and the Hammonds both to do it. He never tried to prevent Mr. Donahue from doing the same, even under the circumstances. He saw the bigger picture. He saw it spreading the art. Every one of them, Mr. And Mrs. Hammond, Mr. Terry, and Mr. Donahue, were spreading his taekwondo seed. They were passing on the art he brought over. They, too would create ripples that also would carry on what Master Choi had started. But Master Choi saw my father as his biggest success. He was still spreading his seed almost forty years later. He had continued and persevered when others gave up. He had conquered adversity and triumphed over challenges with justice on his side. My father stood closest to the source, destined to carry on Choi's legacy. Sending him to Pennsylvania forged direct ties to his lineage, preparing him for the day when Choi would no longer be there to guide him.

The most unexpected thing I gained from this life long martial arts journey was the incredible bonds I shared with my instructors, peers, and students. Hanmaum [3] in Korean is translated to mean one heart. It is an interconnected feeling we get when we share the same beliefs and experiences. We both had this feeling with so many of our instructors and students. They all became part of this giant community my father was building, interconnected and interdependent, like one giant family.

The bonds created during our humble beginnings would last a lifetime. Our years of training taught us so many important lessons. Lessons that would follow us and teach us more about taekwondo than we were capable of understanding. We would use these stories to educate and motivate our students. These lessons we would carry forward to our own teachings. We would use these lessons to enable our students to do the same. The lessons from our past would shape our future.

2016

[3] Jee, L.H. (2002). Hanmaeum, One Heart-One mind: A Korean Buddhist Philosophical Basis of Jeong. In: Chung, E.Y..J., Oh, J.S. (eds) Emotions in Korean Philosophy and Religion. Palgrave Studios Comparative East-West Philosophy. Palgrave Macmillan, Cham. Https://doi.org/10.1007/978-3-030-94747_9

"Master Choi, meeting my father and me for coffee."

Chapter Seven - Unforeseen Events

Running a business and being a full-time martial arts consumed much of my father's time and energy. I was still limited in the capacity I was able to help. He taught six days a week, stayed late to continue his hapkido training, and always made himself available for extra practice with me or anyone in need. He gave much of his time at the school for free. He continued to offer various demonstrations and clinics through out the community at no charge. He had been retired a few years and living out his dream as a full time martial artist and business owner. As a guy who always needed to be busy, he decided to take a part-time job just to occupy his days and create a little extra income. Martial arts classes were mostly evenings, and his job was willing to work around any martial arts events he hosted. He worked part-time as he continued to run the school and promote his business through the community.

Late 2018 I invited my father to attend a seminar and award banquet in Chicago. Dad hated to fly and was reluctant, but I explained we were both eligible to be recognized for our next achievements in hapkido, and we'd get to see a lot of our martial arts friends we had built over the last few years. It happened to work out that we were both eligible at the same time, so I thought it'd be a great opportunity to take advantage, knowing that it may never work out like that again. He agreed, and we traveled to Chicago by plane for the weekend. The weekend was filled with familiar faces from our martial arts past and it was nice to see the friends we had made over the years and discuss our trials and tribulations of owning a martial arts business. We went out for some dinner and drinks the night we arrived to unwind. We talked about the school and the students. We anticipated what the event the next day would be like and what might be expected. It was nice to see my father loosen up and unwind and have a few drinks since he was always busy running the school. We stayed out late and enjoyed the evening. We were walking distance from the hotel, so we walked back to the room to get a good night's sleep for the big day.

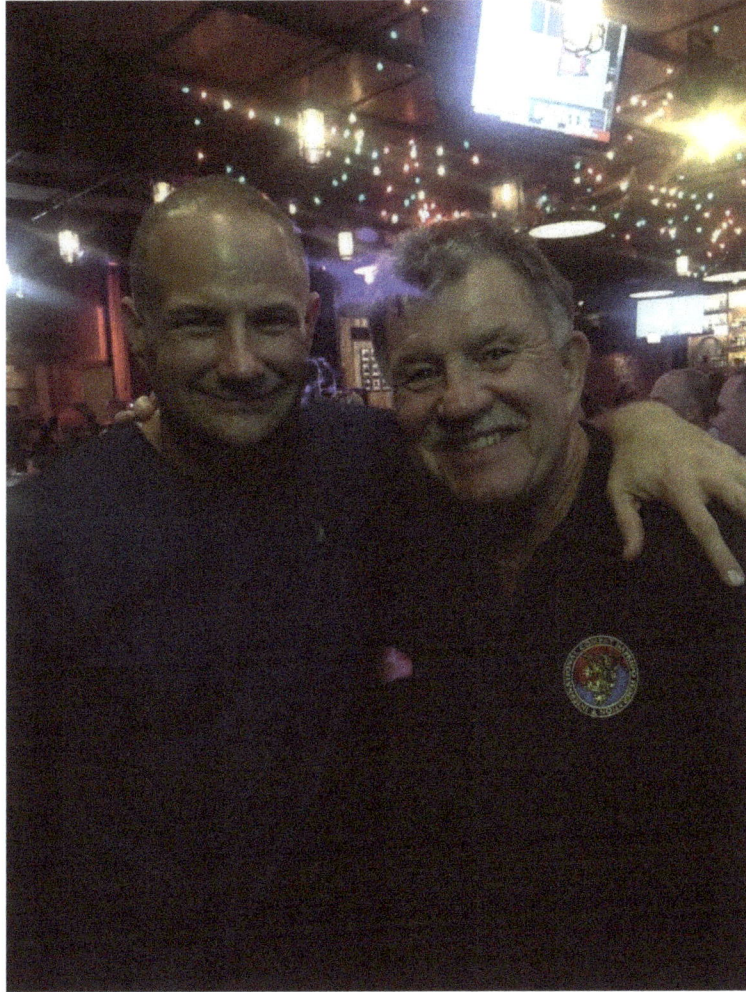

"My father and I during our night out in Chicago."

When we woke, we headed to the event center for an all-day seminar, which would include instructions in stick fighting, pressure points, taekwondo, and hapkido, all done by world-renowned instructors, most of which we knew by name. There was also a karate class and a discussion with a famous actor. My father and I were partners all day together at the seminar. He was 72 years old but letting me throw him and rolling around on the floor like a youngster. We had often paired up at events, but this time was different. We had a great time together. It was just him and I learning together again. I accidentally hit his glasses, executing a technique, and sent them flying across the room. His glasses were bent, and a piece of the frame had broken off. He put the lopsided frame back on his face and joked about it as we resumed our training. Broken glasses didn't prevent him from finishing this full day of training. Both exhausted, we headed back to the room for a shower and some rest before the award banquet. As we rode the elevator to the reception, I noticed him engrossed in his phone, searching for something with an air of secrecy. Curious, I subtly tried to peek at his screen. He appeared to be researching something he didn't want me to see. We headed down to the gala and enjoyed an amazing event. There was a photo booth as we entered. There were rows of fancy tables. A stage was set up for the awards celebration. We searched the premises, looking for a few familiar faces. We bumped into many of our martial arts friends from around the world including some new ones we met earlier that day at the seminar. We waited our turn to get on stage and be recognized in front of our peers in this martial arts community. The event was a success and one we would never forget.

"My father and I at awards gala in Chicago."

A few months later, it was spring. I headed over to my parents' house on a Sunday afternoon for our weekly visit. I often frequented their house with my children, especially in the spring and summer, to use the pool and spend some family time together. My sisters usually visited them too. My children and my sisters would also come to visit their grandparents when everyone was in town. This day was like many others until my father gathered us all together in the kitchen because he needed to tell us all something. We gathered around to listen. He explained that the cancer had returned. We were surprised. He looked so heathy and was always so active. He ran a martial arts school full-time and worked a part-time job. He explained there were few options, and the doctor was recommending radical surgery. We were all surprised because things had been going so well for so long. He added that the doctor recommended acting quickly because of the progression of his cancer. There were lots of tears in the room, but my father was very optimistic. I could tell he was scared, but he stayed positive for all of us, and he had a plan. He also informed us that his doctors had suspected the cancer had returned for quite some time now. I was especially surprised by the news, seeing how he didn't say a word until now. I realized then what he had been researching on our trip just six months earlier. I assumed he did not say anything to not detract from the weekend's excitement. He had participated in all the weekend's events in his condition, knowing what was going on inside him. He had not said a word to me about it. I don't know if I should have been mad at him for allowing me to throw him around or impressed that he was able to do all those activities in his condition. He had suspected it had returned almost a year earlier but wasn't able to get a definite test until now. The insurance company was denying the necessary testing. He was frustrated and unable to get the care he desperately needed because the insurance company deemed it unnecessary at the time. He had finally, after a year, convinced the insurance company to complete the necessary testing. The result was conclusive. The cancer had returned.

He began his second battle with cancer. He scheduled his surgery as soon as possible, which was four months later. He spent only two days in the hospital. He called me to pick him up and give him a ride home. It was sad seeing him struggle to get into the car after just working with him at the seminar a year earlier. He was always my source of strength, and I hated to see him weak and not himself. We arrived at his house, and I assisted him up the steps and into the house. He asked about the business and acted like the taekwondo school was his priority.

He had several instructors at the school that stepped up and helped out with classes. One was a retired gentleman who had practiced with my father for five years. Being retired, he volunteered to help with the early classes. Another female instructor had been with my father since he was with Mr. Donahue. She had followed him to the new location and was the highest-ranking student besides the two of us. She had offered to help with the later classes. Other black belt instructors offered to help whenever they could. All were unpaid. I continued to teach the three hapkido classes and tried to get out early two other days a week to help with some of the taekwondo classes and manage the business end of things. The school functioned but was not the same. They energy he brought to the dojang was missing. His helpers were doing as much as they could to help out, but the place lacked his loud, confident, authoritative voice. I tried to get there more but my work schedule wouldn't allow for it. It was apparent to me he needed to return as soon as possible.

The same evening he arrived home from his surgery, my father ended up in unexpected amounts of pain later that night. Feeling he should not be this uncomfortable, he headed to the emergency room. There were complications from his surgery, and he would have to be admitted. He was in excruciating pain, and there was little the doctors could do for him. The surgery had caused another problem that was creating his pain. He stayed in the hospital for a few days while they tried to just relieve his symptoms. They couldn't address this new problem because his surgery was so recent and not yet healed. I went to visit, and immediately, even in pain, the conversation turned to taekwondo and how the business was doing. It was surviving but a very different place without him. I told him everything was fine. He would eventually return home knowing that he would need another surgery to repair this complication. After returning home, he called all his instructors to see how classes were going. He spent the next couple months with tubes hanging out of his body to relieve his pain while he awaited another surgery. They needed to wait until he was one hundred percent healed before addressing any other issues.

In the hospital or at home, he was always more concerned about the school and his students than his own health. He was constantly calling his instructors daily to check on things. He touched base with me every day to hear about the status of the business. Classes were covered, but no new students were calling or stopping in. His constant activity in the community, teaching at schools, conducting self-defense clinics, and hosting events had stopped because he was unable to be there. He was no longer in the community promoting his business, so things slowed down.

Several months later, his body was healed enough, so he returned to have his second surgery. They needed to operate to address these new complications. They did the necessary repair and then closed up the area that had had the temporary tube hanging from it. Recovery took a little longer this time because his body had been so traumatized from these back-to-back surgeries. Upon returning home talk quickly turned to martial arts. I assured him things would be fine. We all had hoped he would return once his body healed from the first surgery, but this complication would significantly delay his return.

Early in 2020, we received word that Master Choi had passed away. He was our mentor and our friend. He had become very close to my father since he had opened the school. My father and I were devastated. He had done so much over the years to help us and our training would never again be the same. My father would miss his coffee talks and wisdom.

While my father was at home recovering, COVID-19 forced a mandatory shutdown of gyms, including martial arts schools. I was tasked with locking the doors of school and notifying the students. I posted an update on Facebook to inform everyone, uncertain of how long it would be before we could reopen. Knowing what a detriment this could be for my father's business I struggled to find ways to keep his business afloat until he was well enough to return. I set up a live feed from the school and offered free video classes in both taekwondo and hapkido. The classes ran similar to in-person classes starting with some stretching and kicking drills. We then practiced some poomsae and then moved to self-defense techniques. One of the other instructors volunteered to help. Each week, we set up a video camera in the dojang and aired our content to all my father's students. The hope was to keep students engaged until the pandemic was over and we could resume in-person classes. We offered new content with the ability to practice at home with a simple replay of any one of the videos. I tried to cater to both beginners and advanced students. These live feeds went on for a few weeks until the other instructor no longer wanted to join me for fear of getting COVID-19. I had two students reach out and volunteer to take her place. Rather than go to the empty dojang, I set up a stage on my back deck and offered the lessons from my backyard with the assistance of these two students. This didn't last very long before interest in the videos died down. I reached out to students still tuning in and offered to do one-on-one video conferencing or video messaging with any of them privately instead. Despite my efforts, the live videos slowly lost viewership and ultimately came to an end.

I sat wondering for weeks what this would mean for my father's business. I wondered when my father would be able to open, and when he did, would any of his students return? The students all loved my father, and they loved his classes, but would any be motivated to return after months of inactivity? Furthermore, would he be available to run it when that day arrives? My father struggled to pay his rent for a vacant building for several months while he remained at home recovering. He wasn't well enough to work his part-time job. He had no income from the business since none of his students were attending any longer. His cancer started racking up medical bills, and he was worried about how to pay for a retail space that he was unable to use and no longer generated any income.

He and my mother pondered about what the future would hold. Due to his recent surgery and complications that followed, they wondered if he'd ever be able to return. He may be well enough to run the business, but he wasn't sure if he'd ever be able to kick again. If he was well enough to return and run the business, would he physically be able to do what was required to be able to teach again? After much deliberation, they decided it'd be in everyone's best interest to close the school for good. He set up a live Facebook feed from his home and solemnly declared to his students the permeant closure of the school. The announcement stirred a wave of reactions on Facebook, with former students expressing concern and sadness. The decision garnered an overwhelming response of comments and views. Focusing on his health and recovery, he resolved to step away from teaching martial arts, feeling his dream had once again come to an end.

Chapter Eight - Slow Road to Recovery

My sister and I emptied the dojang of all its belongings. She took some of the fitness equipment while I kept most of the martial arts supplies and equipment. I stored in my basement as much as I could fit. I figured I would sell it off and give my father any monies that it generated. The equipment was well worn, and the uniforms were already screen-printed with his logo so I knew there'd be little value. My sister and I threw out or gave away anything we couldn't keep or fit in my basement. It was a sad day for all. Many of the students stopped in to say their final goodbyes to the place. Several came dressed in uniform to get one last picture of the place that brought them so much joy.

My father returned to the surgeon for a follow-up. The doctor asked how he was feeling, and he responded, "Much better." My father was never one to complain. He would find the good in the situation. He asked the doctor about returning to activity and the doctor explained that he needed to find a new normal and the activities that he did before he would not be able to do any longer. My father asked about running again. The doctor respectfully and politely said let's see how things go because I'm not sure that's a great idea. My father was a marathon runner before he got into martial arts. He got me into running, and we ran many 3, 4, and 5-mile fun runs together over the years. My father had hoped not to run a marathon, but hoped he might return to an activity he once enjoyed. He was a guy that was not used to sitting still all day. His doctor wanted to make sure the surgery was a success, so he sent my father for some additional testing to make sure the cancer was successfully removed. They had removed the entire organ and surrounding lymph nodes just like recommended, so this was just to be sure they got it all. So, my father had the test done that day. He waited for a week and took another drive back down to hear the results. The doctor explained that he still had cancer. It was somewhere in his body but they couldn't be sure where. My father was upset and concerned. He had this radical surgery that altered his life forever to get rid of cancer. This wasn't supposed to happen. The doctor explained that it likely traveled and moved because they didn't act quickly enough. The insurance company was to blame for dragging its feet in the beginning on the necessary testing.

My father was a warrior and wouldn't let this get him down. He simply asked what the next course of action was and how he was to proceed. The doctor recommended a new drug on the market. He claimed this pill had extended the lives of many of his patients and hoped it would do the same for my father. He wrote the prescription, and my father headed to the pharmacy to get started as soon as possible. Upon arriving at the pharmacy, he proceeded to pick up his prescription, and the pharmacist told him the costs were over ten thousand dollars a month. My father, not sure what he heard, tried to clarify, "But what's the co-pay?" The pharmacist mentioned again the cost and the insurance company would not cover the costs. My father responded, "I can't afford that! How can anyone afford that?" Devastated by this news he went home and did research. There must be a generic form or something similar. He spent hours on the internet researching similar drugs and their results. He attempted to find one that was similar but less expensive. He set an appointment to return to the doctor to consider these other medication options.

He met with the surgeon again, who informed him that although he did good research, these other drugs just didn't work as well as the one he prescribed. He would not recommend any of these others because studies have shown this new one to be the most effective. He wanted my father to have the best drug for the best chances of extending his life. My father explained there was no way he could afford this. The surgeon picked up the phone and made a call to the drug company and explained my father's situation. The doctor convinced the drug company that their drug was the best choice for my father, and he was a great candidate and spokesperson for their drug. The doctor personally wanted to see him take that and nothing else because he thought it would do the best. He believed in it. The drug representative was able to find a grant to cover most of the drugs for my father. He was thrilled and couldn't wait to get back and tell everyone. He started taking it immediately.

After the second surgery, my father had other tubes still inserted into his body to help aid in bodily functions. He would still have to return to have these medical devises removed. He set another appointment to return. He admired this doctor so much for helping him out with this life-saving medication. He felt like he really cared. My father returned to the office and had these devices removed. He was moving forward in his healing process finally.

A couple months later, he headed to his primary care physician because he had an infection. Suspicious it might be related to the recent surgeries, they sent him back to the surgeon. He was on antibiotics for a couple weeks, but the infection was internal. Urine was backing up internally between his organs. This was causing the infection. The doctor explained that the radiation treatments he had during his initial diagnosis had caused severe damage to surrounding organs, including his bladder. He would need another surgery to repair the bladder. The doctor explained he would attempt to fix it, but the surrounding tissue was destroyed from the radiation, and they would have to pull good muscle from his leg to be able to repair it. This would mean an incision and removal of a healthy muscle in his leg in an attempt to heal his damaged bladder. This would cause weakness and instability on one side of his body for the rest of his life if he agreed. My father trusted the surgeon and didn't see any other options. It needed to be repaired to prevent further infections.

The surgery was scheduled. My father got a drive back down to the hospital, and surgery took twelve hours. He spent more than a week in the hospital recovering from this repair. He went home, hopeful it would solve the problem. He was having trouble walking because of the missing muscle in the leg but was eager to get back to his woodworking at home and his retail job. After a couple months of recovery the doctor would allow him to return to his hobbies. He would be able to return to work with restrictions. His excessive medical bills made him anxious to return. He loved his work at the retail store. Returning gave him purpose. They were excited to see him back and willingly worked around his limitations.

He would get another infection just a couple months later and have to return to the doctor's office to have another scan. They needed to determine if that last surgery was successful and what might be causing this new infection. The scan revealed that the good tissue from the leg was not adhering to the already damaged bladder tissue. The surgery was not successful. He asked the doctor for the next course of action. He was running out of options. The doctor explained that they could go back in and attempt to reconstruct the bladder again, but there was less than a fifty percent chance it would be successful as there was no good tissue there. The second option was they could remove it altogether, and he would have an ostomy bag for the rest of his life. My father was not thrilled with either option. The success rate of the surgery was a huge risk to his already battered body, but the thought of his quality of life with an ostomy bag seemed less than acceptable.

He decided he would have the surgery to remove the bladder and adjust his life accordingly. He no longer did martial arts and didn't have the business any longer, so he would cope. The retail store would accommodate as needed. He was happy to be alive, and given the chance with this new drug, he wouldn't let a little baggie get him down.

The surgery went well, and he had to adjust his life somewhat. Certain things like swimming would be less enjoyable. He overcame and preserved. He had this indomitable spirit that guided him through all these obstacles, and he continued to be on top of this illness. Infections would become a regular thing, but he kept his spirits high and never let it get him down. He was happy to be alive and it showed in his every action.

Chapter Nine - The Legacy

Late Spring 2020, I received a call from one of my hapkido students looking to train. He was out of work because his business was forced to shut down, and he was going nuts being home with the kids and his wife. He called, hoping I could figure something out before he drove himself crazy. Like so many other individuals during the pandemic, the confinement was taking its toll mentally and emotionally. The idea of being home every day with the family and wife with no money and no place to go was a recipe for disaster. I explained to him that we weren't supposed to be practicing at all because the state forced us to shut down and maintain 6 feet at all times. I explained I didn't agree with the laws but had to abide by them. He asked if just he and I could practice together a couple days a week so he could remain involved. This student had been one of the volunteers who helped create Facebook live videos at the dojang when the pandemic began. Later, he assisted me in the backyard, trying to keep the school alive with online classes. Feeling indebted to him, I agreed to teach him twice a week in my basement, off the grid. I instructed him to keep our lessons private, as I didn't want word to get out. I figured working with one healthy person who had been in isolation for weeks would be harmless. He began immediately. He was thrilled to be back at it. I could see a sigh of relief in his face just being able to get out of his house for a couple hours. My basement was super small and not adequate space but we made the most of it. It reminded me of my beginning days with the Hammonds in their basement. Two weeks later, I received another call from another former hapkido student. He called just to check in and have someone to talk to. He stated how much he, too missed our classes. He was a man who lived alone and, too, became bored being home alone with his dogs. I mentioned that I was working on one with his fellow student. Immediately, he wanted to join. He was anxious to get started and rushed over to the basement to join in. Our two classes a week became a regular thing. The basement was crowded with just three of us. We really didn't have space to adequately practice anything. So we moved practices outside to the backyard. It was spring outside, and we had much more space. However, my yard had uneven terrain, which made for difficult practice in shoes. We made the most of it for several weeks.

My phone rang again and a couple of my father's taekwondo students reached out to ask if I'd continue to send them videos so they could continue to practice and progress. I sent the videos they requested and followed up in a day or two. I offered live Zoom classes for others to still be able to continue their progress. I was still working full-time through the pandemic since my business was deemed essential. I conducted classes in person at my house and video and Zoom sessions in the evenings and on the weekends. I seemed busier than ever teaching and was happy to keep the spirit alive. I offered these sessions at no charge. I was just happy to have some students.

Within a couple weeks, several other students reached out to me. All were frustrated with the pandemic and the state's way of handling it. I wanted to be able to help them not only with their martial arts but also give them a way to cope with the confinement and isolation they were all experiencing. I was concerned about getting shut down by the state if word got out and my basement was not big enough anymore. If I had large groups of people at my house practicing in my yard regularly, I would surely have the neighbors reporting me.

One of the students called and offered up his camp. It was a barn out in the country and off the grid, and surely no one would know we were there. I made phone calls to everyone who had reached out and offered to teach as long as no one mentioned it. It would be our own *Fight Club*. We all signed waivers admitting we understood the health risks involved and agreed to practice and waive all rights.

I drove my father's old mats out with some pads and bags. We got started right away. Everyone who agreed showed up even though the barn was located 25 minutes outside of town. We had a blast and reviewed techniques we all had learned prior to the shutdown. The barn had a leaky roof, so the mats were wet whenever it rained. Our daily routine involved mopping the mats off when we arrived to clean off the mud and debris. Classes were often interrupted by insects and mice running across the mats while we were practicing. The barn had a spray-painted name on the side, Rattlesnake Barn. I first thought it was a joke to scare off neighbors. The owner assured me there were really rattlesnakes in the high weeds next to the barn and I should be careful. He claimed the high weeds near the building were their hiding place, and he had encountered several. He said he cut the areas near the barn regularly to keep them visible. I didn't believe him, and we all laughed about it as we went into practice.

"Photo of rattlesnake in the road outside of Rattlesnake barn"

Several of us carpooled because of the distance to the barn. The two guys who started in my basement lived nearby me, so we often drove together. Our car ride was filled with the excitement of secret barn practices. Our lessons were hidden from the public and not discussed with anyone. We felt like the Hwarang[4] learning in private from monks. Our discussions also consisted of our daily life struggles. Everyone had financial troubles from the pandemic, and there was no relief in sight. Our classes provided a temporary relief from everyone's daily struggles. Our time in the car often seemed like a group psychology session as we all shared our concerns.

The barn was a success and ran all of the summer. We ran classes just like we would in a dojang and even had flags hung on the wall. One night, upon leaving, several cars stopped in the middle of this old country road. It was unusual to see any traffic on these back country roads. I stopped to see what was holding up traffic. Everyone was out of their cars, standing with their cameras, taking pictures of a rattlesnake over 6 feet long laying in the middle of the road. The

---

[4] Michael A. Demarco, MA.
Taekwondo, The Korean Martial Art,
Via Media Publishing Company
2016

snake stopped traffic both ways. Everyone took pictures to marvel over its mammoth size and stopped to count the rattlers.

At the end of summer, the owner rented out the space to a boat company for winter storage, so I had to find another space. I searched around and couldn't find anything affordable. I only had eight students and couldn't afford much. With the pandemic, there were lots of vacant spaces, but every landlord was trying to recoup lost revenues. My friend Mike offered to help. I considered Mike, my friend. He had started at Murray's Family Martial Arts Center with me in hapkido after enrolling his grandchildren and nephews in taekwondo classes. He was one of the first to contact me during the pandemic and come to my basement to practice. He also accompanied me in the carpooling. Mike talked to a friend of his and found a small retail space that was not occupied. It was on a side street in an abandoned storage building and was perfect not to be noticed. I was still concerned the state might find out and shut things down. I gathered the equipment from the barn and brought it back to my house to clean it all. Everything was filthy from the leaky barn. The mats were soiled with mud. All the bags and kicking shields needed to be hosed down. Mike came over and spent his whole Sunday outside with me, pressure washing all the equipment. Once cleaned, I packed up all the mats and equipment again and brought them to our new space. Once all set up, I invited my mother and father to show them the new location. I knew it was not as large or as nice as my father's dojang, but I hoped it would be adequate for the time being. Both my parents were excited to see me keep the spirit alive. My father was still having trouble walking from his surgeries, and he kept having regular infections, but he was healing.

We took safety precautions at the new school. We used sanitizer before and after any contact. We adhered to the mandatory mask laws. We abided by one golden rule, "If you are sick or anyone in your house is sick, you do not come to class until everyone is better." Everyone was really good about this because no one wanted to get the others sick.

I continued to receive calls from several of my father's former taekwondo students looking to get back into it. The new school was nothing in size compared to what my father had previously created, but it was a place for me to try to feel whole again and fill a void in my life. My father was thrilled about the new school opening. Talks at his house quickly returned to that of taekwondo. He was mentally and emotionally supportive and so happy to see me continue. Although, I could tell he wanted to be right there doing it with me. He started to get the itch again. His surgeries had prevented him from doing most activities. He was no longer able to run. He wasn't able to swim. He did walk every day, but the missing muscles in his leg still created balance and stability issues, so his leg fatigued easily. He had not been practicing taekwondo in quite some time now. I didn't see him ever being well enough to return.

All of my students were former students of my father's school. I didn't advertise at all, so I didn't attract any new students, just the ones he had previously. We had fun and learned a lot, even if it was very different from what everyone was used to. I decided to only offer classes for adults and teenagers. I remembered the old days with the Hammonds and how much more fun it was for me. I still missed the hard-core training methods from those days. I planned to return to my roots. I decided to combine taekwondo and hapkido together into one class. My work schedule still limited the time I had available. I didn't want to lose either taekwondo or hapkido students by only offering one. Plus, my years of training taught me that these two arts overlapped in more ways than they were different. I would combine the two curriculums to make it work in my limited time availability.

I had nine students at most which filled the small retail space I rented. A few left, and when they did, I would receive another call from one of my father's previous students looking to get back into it. I struggled to keep the room filled, but no matter how many showed up, I loved to teach and share my knowledge. Martial arts was still a hobby. There were hopes of making it into more, but my work schedule would not allow it.

After two years at the new location, I decided to host a small Christmas party at my home for all my students. Grateful for their presence in my life, I wanted to show my appreciation. We enjoyed food and drinks, engaging in lively conversation in a social setting outside of our usual routine. It reminded me of the parties my father would host for all his instructors and students. I wanted all students to know they were family to me. We had helped one another through the pandemic by bonding in something we all shared and loved, martial arts.

My mother and father attended the party to support me and my efforts. Everyone was glad to see my father after all he'd been through. Most followed his progress on social media and knew of his condition. He was doing better after so many serious health problems. My father asked everyone to come into the same room. He gathered everyone around because he had an announcement to make. All of my students gather close to listen. My father often offered words of wisdom to his students when they checked in from time to time. We all expected one of his life lessons. He stood up in front of everyone at the party and exclaimed that in just one month, he intended to return to classes. He said he would return in whatever capacity he was capable of. He would return to assist me in instruction. He knew my job often caused me to cancel classes or delay starting times. He wanted to be able to help me succeed. He wanted to be a bigger part of the school again. I was thrilled, and so were all his students. We anxiously awaited his return.

He had multiple surgeries in the last couple of years. He had organs removed. He had muscles torn from his leg. He had been in and out of the hospital as a result of complications, but he still intended to return. I think he wanted to prove to himself he could still do it. I realized that it was more than that. It was a way he and I could continue to do something together we loved. Early 2023, he did return.

He came in to cover classes whenever I couldn't be there. He showed up two days a week to assist in instruction. He showed up and offered priceless wisdom and knowledge to me and all my students. He continued to guide me on this journey that he started so many years ago.

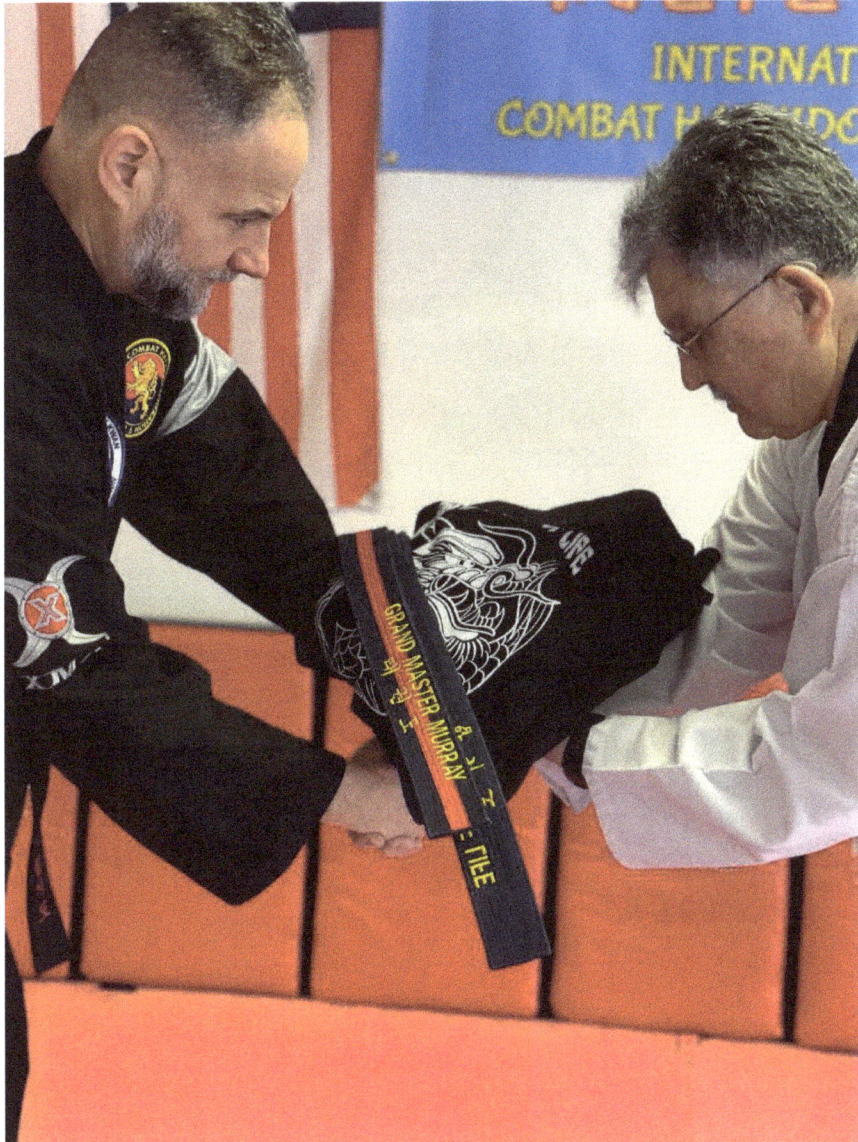

"My father's return to the dojang after his illness."

My father had several former students call periodically to check in with him during the years he was away. Many felt such a connection they would call or message him about his health and offer prayers. He even had several students who stopped by the house and continued to check on him and his health. Of course, for anyone who called or stopped by, he referred them to the new school and encouraged them to return, and several did. One day, he received a call from Mr Harris. He had practiced with us at the Hammond's old school. After a short conversation and a few text messages, he managed to coax Mr. Harris, at age 77, to return. Mr. Harris was excited to get back into taekwondo and immediately started working towards his next belt. He was surprised to see we still offered hapkido as part of the curriculum. It was weird at first because he was the higher rank when we began. Now, I was the teacher to this guy I looked up to and admired so early in my journey. I just thought where he'd be at rank-wise had he continued. Mr. Harris had followed Mr. Donahue when he took over Master Choi's school with the intention of continuing. Mr Harris told me that with no explanation Mr. Donahue told him he was no longer welcome there at his school. At that time, Upstate Taekwondo and Hapkido was the only taekwondo school around so he had no other places to go to train. Mr. Harris had stopped practicing but never lost the desire. Now, he was able to continue. I also learned that Mr. Donahue had specifically told Mr. and Mrs. Locke they, too, were not welcome at Upstate Taekwondo and Hapkido and that's why they had stopped practicing. I never knew any of this. I wondered why Mr. Donahue had discouraged all these black belt instructors from Choi's from following him when he opened Upstate Taekwondo and Hapkido. Instructors who had taught my father and I so many life lessons through taekwondo were asked not to return, and we'd never know why. Possibly, he felt threatened by having so many other high ranking black belts around. We weren't sure.

One day, my father came to work privately with Mr. Harris on the weekend and he noticed me practicing material for my next hapkido test in the back. He came up to me and offered to help in any way he could. His body was battered and beaten down from cancer, but he wanted to help me succeed. He had trouble maintaining his balance due to all those surgeries, but he was more concerned about me and my progression. He was limited in the amount of bending and movement he was capable of, but he showed up every day to contribute in any way he could. As he put aside time expecting to help me prepare for my next time I instead helped him prepare for his next belt. He was in his late seventies, but he continued to make progress toward his next level. Limited in his abilities from all his surgeries, he demonstrated the warrior spirit and continued to forge ahead.

I made plans to attend another seminar in Chicago with my wife , who also recently joined martial arts. I wasn't sure if my father would be well enough to travel. I asked anyway, not sure what he'd say. He had been my partner in this lifelong journey with me and the event wouldn't be the same without him. I hoped he would be able but I didn't want him to attend if he wasn't feeling up to it. He took a day to think about it but texted me and said he'd be there. He agreed to attend with my wife and me. We all boarded a plane for Chicago and decided to make a weekend of it. We did some sightseeing and lots of walking. He was a trooper and didn't complain once about the excessive walking. He seemed to be having a great time. We had some great meals and adventures in a short few days. We attended the seminar and continued to increase our knowledge base. This was my wife's first seminar, and she was filled with excitement. She and I worked together. My father jumped in any time he could. My father, limited in the activities he was able to do, was a sponge absorbing all the things he could take back to the students. He couldn't wait to return and share his knowledge. Over the weekend, he mentioned that he thought he might have the start of another infection because he started to have symptoms again. We returned home the following day.

"My father, my wife (Nicole), and I attending a seminar together in Chicago 2023."

The infection had returned, and he ended up in the hospital shortly after we returned. We learned from the doctors he had developed a hernia from one of the prior surgeries that was causing another blockage somewhere in his system. This blockage was causing the infection. The doctors pondered all the options and were reluctant to operate again. He remained in the hospital for a few days, awaiting a verdict on what could be done. My father's concern was that he wouldn't make it to class that night to open the school. I assured him everything would be okay and he should worry about getting better. After a couple days, he was sent home with a plan to have it addressed at a later date with his cancer doctor. The later date got pushed up because, within two weeks of his release, he was again having pain from the blockage. He needed the surgery soon. The doctor scheduled a day and time to get it done right away. A mesh lining had come loose from his earlier surgery and caused his most recent problems. They would have to operate and rebuild the abdomen lining. He wanted to let me and all the students know he wouldn't be there that day, but he expected to return the day after the surgery. The doctor did the surgery and put him on restrictive duties. He wasn't able to shovel or bend. He wouldn't be allowed to operate a snow blower. He wasn't able to return to work. He was directed to take it easy and rest. He was informed of the severity of the upcoming surgery, given the extensive trauma his body had already endured. The doctor warned him that if he didn't take it easy, further damage might be irreversible. Despite this, he showed up to class the following night, determined not to let anything interfere with his taekwondo training.

My father continued to persevere through all his obstacles. He showed up and continued his training and earned his master's level in hapkido soon after. He was determined to not let cancer win. His driving force was returning to his students. He had returned to fulfill the legacy.

Chapter Ten - Ripples In the Pond

Taekwondo is a Korean self-defense art with roots dating back over 2000 years. The literal translation means the way of the hand and foot. However, over its long history, taekwondo has taken on many different forms. It has adapted countless times to meet the needs of the Korean people. Subak [5] was one of the earliest documented forms of these fighting arts that originated in China. Subak was a fighting art used by the military distinctively for combat. Many Koreans fled Korea to avoid the Japanese armies and originally practiced their arts in other countries, including China. This early version would make its way back to Korea and later be called tangsoodo meaning the way of China hand, based on the original karate style learned in China. Taekyon was another of these art forms, along with lineage to taekwondo. This art closely resembled dance. It was initially taught as a game. This same art would later evolve into a fighting art with links to criminal activities. It became an early fighting system used by gangsters in the streets of Korea to keep order. As a result it lacked any moral code and values. These early art forms, among others, would later lead to the art known today as taekwondo, each contributing to the evolution in different ways. Combative arts used by military sources in those days would serve different purposes than martial arts do today. This evolution was caused by a change in the needs of the Korean people. What began as private training to avoid the Japanese would become an art that the Koreans would turn into a competitive sport attracting participants from around the world.

The Hwarang [6] was a group of noble warriors that arose from Korea during the Japanese occupation. Known for their fighting skills, these soldiers practiced hand-to-hand combat as learned from the ancient fighting arts, long before the development of taekwondo. They were taught in private by Buddhist monks. These knights were known for their bravery in battle. They were known for their courage. They were known for their faithfulness to their friends. They were

---

[5] Michael A. Demarco, MA.
Taekwondo, The Korean Martial Art,
Via Media Publishing Company
2016
[6] Michael A. Demarco, MA.
Taekwondo, The Korean Martial Art,
Via Media Publishing Company
2016

known for their warrior spirit. The Buddhist monks served as mentors for the Hwarang in both physical and spiritual ways, for these warriors. Although fierce in battle, they developed a foundation of ethics based on Buddhist philosophy. These core values served as a basis for martial arts, like taekwondo, that later followed. Although a strong military force, the Hwarang[7] adhered to these core values even in battle.

There is a common thread that has stayed in tack throughout these thousands of years of adaptations. It is filial piety. There was an allegiance among its practitioners that created bonds. There was a sense of duty and devotion creating loyalty among its followers.

Master Choi brought his art, tangsoodo, to the United States. He started practicing this art as a child in school in Korea and continued into adulthood. This art that he learned was rich in heritage. It provided both practical military application and a moral compass. It had a core set of values and moral guidelines different from those of its taekyon[8] ancestors. For Master Choi, his art took on a deeper meaning. It served as a means of personal growth and development. This is the art he brought to the United States; tangsoodo was just one of the names of similar arts that existed prior to the unification under the taekwondo name. Under the unification taekwondo would later become the Korean national sport as featured in the Olympics. The Korean government unified similar karate styles under the taekwondo name to be able to promote worldwide. They were very proud of their national sport and wanted to make it available for the world to see. They did it as taekwondo. To Master Choi, it was more than a sport; it was his way of life. He brought taekwondo to this country to be able to share his culture and upbringing with the American people. He wanted to build a community from the virtues of his art. His intent was to pass on the Hwarang spirit. The unification would increase the popularity but change some of the essence of the art. Master Choi welcomed the changes as it was good for taekwondo but he would embrace his proud heritage for the values it instilled. Looking back, I realized that the reason he rarely taught us new materials was not because he didn't want to teach us. It wasn't

---

[7] Michael A. Demarco, MA.
Taekwondo, The Korean Martial Art,
Via Media Publishing Company
2016
[8] Michael A. Demarco, MA.
Taekwondo, The Korean Martial Art,
Via Media Publishing Company
2016

because his English wasn't great. It was because he was attempting to create a network of individuals that would carry forth his taekwondo teachings. He enabled his instructors to teach and spread the knowledge, knowing he would not always be around. His expectations were that his network carry on the purpose of taekwondo as he intended it. He wanted them to share the many benefits of taekwondo with generations to follow. The rewards of taekwondo are abundant and designed to benefit all. The sports aspects of taekwondo are flashy and appealing to many. It pushes its practitioners to perform better and sets a high bar for all physical components of the sport, but our bodies age. Our flexibility declines. Our speed and timing slowly diminish no matter how hard we practice. The competitive nature of the sport is not for all. The longer we study the physical aspect of art, the more we realize the mind controls every aspect of our lives, including our bodies. Taekwondo trains us first in the physical aspects, but practicing for a lifetime trains the mind.

Taekwondo continues to evolve. Each taekwondo group or organization has its own focus. All are good in their own way. Some focus more on the sport and competition, while others focus more on self-defense. Some are very militant in nature, while others are more casual. Some embrace the core values and principles more than others. All create exceptional bonds amongst their practitioners. All serve a purpose. I was lucky enough to find one that made me a better person and, in the process, created these unforgettable bonds with others, including my own father.

I know now that deep down, my father always wanted me to take over the school and fulfill our Taekwondo & Pizza to Go dream. I appreciated that and always wanted the same but deemed it not realistic because of my full time job. I missed the fact that the dream was never about the school itself; it was about me. It was never about the physical school for him. He built the school over and over. It was his way to spend time with his son while fulfilling our dream. I was too self-consumed in moving to the next level and learning something new that I missed what he learned early on. It was about the bonds. It was about the families. It was about sharing with others the fire that burned deep within us both.

As a teenager, I started my martial arts journey solely to learn self-defense. My renewed interest in my twenties may have been a direct result of my father's nagging and encouragement, but I quietly rode on the coattails of this man I looked up to and admired dearly, not because he was my father, but because he had set out to pioneer the path we only spoke of jokingly in our beginning days. The dream was to run our own school together some day. I initially thought his love of the art and desire to pass on his passion was what solely motivated him to achieve all his goals and pursue his dreams, but somewhere along the way, I realized that it was the Dad in him just trying to fulfill that dream of his son so many years earlier. He had never given up on our dream of running a school together. What I never realized was that his drive to complete this dream together had created this unbreakable bond between him and me. We shared a love that allowed us to create a martial arts community around us. A love that allowed us to share our vast and ever-growing knowledge with others for over forty years. We did it while running a school together. We both earned high ranks in several disciplines, but the true reward was spending time together doing it along the way. We spent time together doing something we were both passionate about. The countless extra classes he dedicated to my return weren't just so I could learn and catch up. It was time well spent with his son building a legacy. The hours devoted to learning and practicing new materials together over the years built a relationship that I truly treasure. We had spent days away at tournaments and training seminars, sharing our passion but creating this unique bond. We attended conferences and awards banquets for each other over the years encouraging and supporting each other's accomplishments. My father was not only there physically and emotionally to support me and my accomplishments; he was part of the hard work that went into creating them. He was the fuel and fire behind my martial arts success. I realize that many young men and women share an interest in sports or hobbies with their parents. Some even try to live vicariously through one another as their kids learn to play sports or take on the family's special interests, but I have had the opportunity to share my love every day together with the man I still look up to and admire. My father did not live vicariously through me as a teen. He did it with me. He went through all the same paces and struggles. We have trained together for over 40 years. I spent countless hours week after week doing something I truly love with someone to whom I owe everything. It was never the family business, as we both kept day jobs. It was an activity that we made time for together around our full time jobs and separate from our family responsibilities. My father made special time for me whenever I needed it over the years, and he did it through martial arts. Martial arts has proven to be much more to me than an activity or hobby. It has proven to be my safe space when I need it. It has provided a pleasant distraction from life's struggles and challenges some days. It has served as a mental reset when needed. Some days it's just a fun activity and time with others. Thanks to my father, the dojang remains my favorite place to be, regardless of what's happening in my life. Over the years, I've formed friendships and strong bonds with fellow instructors and students, but none compare to the relationship I've cultivated with my own father.

He has taught me how to be a better man. He taught me how to be a better parent. He taught me how to be a better brother and son. He taught me how to value and cultivate my relationships. He made me a better worker. He made me into a leader. He did all this without me knowing. He did it through his taekwondo lessons. The experiences I gained from this journey with my father made me successful in every aspect of my life, not just in martial arts.

People join a martial arts program for so many different reasons. Some start as I did for self-defense needs. Many are attracted by discipline and self-control. Some are drawn in by the competition. Others join to become more physically fit. While others try because of a friend or relative. Some do it to reach the goal of being a black belt one day. The benefits of martial arts are so vast that it would be impossible to list all the physical, mental, and emotional benefits. At any different time during my 40-year journey if you had asked me what I got out of it or why I continued to practice, my answer would have been different each time. For me it served a purpose in my life in so many different ways at so many different times. In the good times and the bad, martial arts were there for me.

What had started-off as a choice of a scared, traumatized teenager turned into a lifetime journey of self-discovery, one which shaped my future from that day forward. One simple choice to learn self-defense and be prepared for a potential repeat event that would never happen again empowered me to become the man I am today. What started-off as an unfortunate event for me as a child, resulted in the greatest bond a son could ever have with his father. The shame and resentment I felt over being-beaten as a child allowed me to choose a path that would shape the rest of my life. I will always remember the event, for it resulted in who I have become. Therefore, looking back, I am grateful for the choice I made. I would never seek revenge but instead be grateful and see this incident as a gift. It gave me this special bond with my father. As he ages, I realize how fortunate I have been to share my journey and passion with my father but, more importantly, the quality time I have been able to spend with him as he grows older, knowing that the day will come when I am no longer to cherish these moments. All this time, I thought it was his passion and his dream. I did not realize until much later that it was always my dream and my passion he was fulfilling. His desire was selfless and about his only son. The quality time with my father during this lifelong journey we shared would turn out to be the greatest gift I could ever receive. Few people are ever able to live out their childhood dreams. I lived it ever day of my life for the past forty years and did it with someone who I love deeply. This bond I built with my father would prove to be invaluable in my life. I see now how fortunate I was the day he said, "Maybe I'll try." I continue to live and build his legacy.

I've dedicated a lifetime to martial arts and have seen the numerous health benefits, but our bodies deteriorate. I have experienced many mental benefits and physical ones. I have seen benefits at my job. I learned how to set goals and achieve them. I learned how to be a leader. I became empowered as a manager at work through martial arts. It helped me keep a clear head to be able to guide me through family and relationship obstacles along the way.

As I age, I continue to see the spiritual benefits of the arts. Call it Ki (Chi) or aura, life force, God or whatever you like to define it as, but this force has motivated my father to get up after being knocked down by cancer multiple times. He embodies the warrior spirit. He is fierce in his battle against cancer. He is faithful to his friends and family. He is noble and true. He has the courage to keep getting up after being knocked down. He continues to live the tenets in every aspect of his life. His motivation and driving force is that his job is not done. His students still need him. They all still seek his knowledge and wisdom, including me. His resilience proves to be an inspiration to us all. My father, who dedicated the last 40 years of his life, still continues today to pursue Murray's Taekwondo and Pizza to Go dream. This pursuit has become our way of life. It continues to motivate him whenever he gets knocked down.

Grand Master Murray is not someone you'd see featured in *Black Belt* magazine or *Taekwondo Times*. His name is not a household name in the vast martial arts community, but he has made a giant footprint and legacy in our small community that will last many years after him. He has created thousands of martial arts ripples from his single pebble. Each of these ripples continues to pass on this knowledge and passion to their kids, families, and friends. My father was nominated for numerous Hall of Fame awards several times and has never accepted one. His journey has been about his students and making them into better people. It was never about the glory or recognition. It was about the dream. He has been a true inspiration to all his students and instructors, past and present. My father's legacy and teachings will live on much past him. He invoked passion in his students that will extend for generations to come. He has had several of his previous instructors who went on to open their own schools. The pebble he had cast so many years prior continues to cause ripples. His love for the art has inspired so many and continues to burn like a fire, not only within him, but in everyone he touched over this journey.

Master Choi first cast his pebble into the water. Some of the ripples kept moving while others faded away. The Hammonds were a big reason that my father and I continued with taekwondo. Our early days would set the foundation for the message that taekwondo had for us. We benefitted from all the teachings. The Hammonds were the first to teach us that the true meaning of taekwondo didn't lie merely in the class lessons but was found in the training. This training was not an art of kicking and punching, as we first learned. It was a means of self-discovery. The training was a path to follow along this long road of self-improvement. If it hadn't been for meeting the Hammonds, our journey would have gone differently.

Other ripples Master Choi created would not flourish at all. Some would continue moving, missing the essence of his teachings. Some, like my father, would continue and create their own ripples. My father's legacy would be his success story. My father was the one chosen to carry out taekwondo as it was intended by our instructor, Master Choi. He set forth his legacy that would become our own.

My father successfully ran a martial arts school for twenty-eight years. He had an impact on the members of the community and touched thousands of students. His sole motivator may have been to keep the Murray's Taekwondo and Pizza To Go dream alive but even he didn't realize the impact he would have for generations to come.

Six of Grand Master Murray's students currently run martial arts programs within the community. That's six ripples that he created that are still currently spreading his way. I continue to be one of those ripples, hoping to continue to generate ripples of my own. I proved to be the most successful of the ripples, not because of the number of students that attended but because of the experiences I was fortunate enough to share with him along the way. My school remains small in size compared to the mega school he had created. I learned that as much as I hated to see the introduction of children to taekwondo, it quickly caused the popularity of taekwondo across the country. Limiting my program to adults significantly restricts my marketability, so my school remains small. My father's means of encouraging parents to join with their children was a big part of his success. It not only helped fill the room, but it allowed him to spread the taekwondo spirit throughout each family. Children join for the kicking and punching. They join because their peers are doing it. They join because their parents encourage them to join. They are too young to understand all that taekwondo has to offer. It took my father getting the parents involved for the children to see the bigger picture of what taekwondo could offer them. Each family took my father's teachings to share at home. Taekwondo became a way to overcome their personal struggles together with their families. Every struggle became a lesson on their taekwondo journey. It became their way of life.

This single man selflessly built a community of martial artists that continues to spread his seed and passion. He helped guide individuals and families using the tenets as he taught them. Grand Master Murray created a generation of followers that continue to use taekwondo's guiding principles to instill morals in a society lacking ethics. He continues to make the world a better place, one student at a time, with his efforts. His intentions will impact not only those that he personally touched but those that will continue to be touched by his legacy for generations to come.

Every student, whether still active or not in taekwondo, still remembers the impact my father had on their lives. His teaching shaped each of their lives from that day forward. Those who became teachers under his guidance walk every day knowing that every step they make moving forward was somehow set forth by his teachings. Even those who broke apart from him at one time, their teachings will be forever impacted by their years with Grand Master Murray. Their teachings would never have been the same had they not stepped foot into his dojang and realized the power of his spirit.

Every place I go, I bump into one of my father's previous students. Everyone mentions him and remembers their days at the dojang. Everyone has a story to tell about how he impacted their life in some way. Some stories are exciting and how he empowered them, while others are heartfelt sentiments of something he did to save them from themselves. They all love and adore my father and remember the bond he created with him. When my father returns to the dojang each night to teach, I mention who I bumped into that day. He remembers every single one of them, first name and last. He remembers their rank. He remembers how long they practiced and when they left. He always has an interesting story to share of a struggle they had and how he helped them through it.

However, his biggest success story will always be his son. He is a proud father but I'm more proud of him and all he's done to carry on the legacy and continue to make ripples.

Strength manifests in various ways. Some find it through religion or divine intervention, but for my father, it came through taekwondo. His students became his source of strength. Despite illness, his determination to return to taekwondo remains unwavering. The sense of being valued and needed by his students outweighs any physical setbacks he's had to overcome. He sets his mind on persevering through each obstacle because his students still need him. He built this giant community that depended on him for guidance and strength for forty years, now, he needs them as much as they needed him. His drive to return to classes and continue to live out the legacy, remains stronger than illness. He has a purpose to serve. His students still need him.

Don't ever underestimate the power of the bonds we create throughout our lives. The concept of Jeong [9] is a love that we build with others over time and through experiences. It is a feeling of warmness or closeness we create with others. It defines our loyalty to others. This emotion is unique to Korean culture. My father created this bond of interconnectedness with all his students, joining his mind and heart with theirs through taekwondo, hanmaum.[10]

A Taekwondo Bond; The Spirit Within

---

[9] Jee, L.H. (2002). Hanmaeum, One Heart-One mind: A Korean Buddhist Philosophical Basis of Jeong.
In: Chung, E.Y..J., Oh, J.S. (eds) Emotions in Korean Philosophy and Religion.
Palgrave Studios Comparative East-West Philosophy.
Palgrave Macmillan, Cham.
Https://doi.org/10.1007/978-3-030-94747_9
[10] Jee, L.H. (2002). Hanmaeum, One Heart-One mind: A Korean Buddhist Philosophical Basis of Jeong.
In: Chung, E.Y..J., Oh, J.S. (eds) Emotions in Korean Philosophy and Religion.
Palgrave Studios Comparative East-West Philosophy.
Palgrave Macmillan, Cham.
Https://doi.org/10.1007/978-3-030-94747_9

Bibliography

Jee, L.H. (2002). Hanmaeum, One Heart-One mind: A Korean Buddhist Philosophical Basis of Jeong.
In: Chung, E.Y..J., Oh, J.S. (eds) Emotions in Korean Philosophy and Religion.
Palgrave Studios Comparative East-West Philosophy.
Palgrave Macmillan, Cham.
Https://doi.org/10.1007/978-3-030-94747_9

Michael A. Demarco, MA.
Taekwondo, The Korean Martial Art,
Via Media Publishing Company
2016